CURRICULUM PLANNING AND THE PRIMARY SCHOOL

Keith Morrison worked in primary and secondary education for many years before moving into teacher education. He has been involved in several curriculum development projects for primary schools. His recent publications include: *Improving Reading Comprehension: Approaches and Practices*; *Tensions in Subject Specialist Teaching in Primary Schools*; *Primary School Subject Specialists as Agents of School-Based Curriculum Change*; *School Self-Evaluation: Establishing a New National Consensus?*; *Developing a Framework for Curriculum Cohesion in Primary Teacher Education*; *Problems and Possibilities in Primary Teacher Appraisal*; *The Curriculum From 5−16: a Primary Response*. He is currently a lecturer in primary education at the University of Durham.

Ken Ridley was a headteacher in primary schools before moving into primary teacher education in England, and North and South America, where he has been involved in course development, teaching and evaluation. He is the author of: *The National Primary Survey: a Head's Response*; *Mixed Ability Teaching in the Primary School*; *Primary School Organization: Some Rhetoric and Some Reason* (with D. Trembath). He is presently Head of the Department of Professional Studies at The College of Ripon and York St John, York.

CURRICULUM PLANNING AND THE PRIMARY SCHOOL

KEITH MORRISON and KEN RIDLEY

P·C·P
Paul Chapman
Publishing Ltd

Copyright © 1988 Keith Morrison and Ken Ridley
First published 1988

Paul Chapman Publishing Ltd
144 Liverpool Road
London
N1 1LA

British Library Cataloguing in Publication Data

Morrison, Keith
    Primary school curriculum planning.
    1. Elementary schools—Great Britain—
    Curricula 2. Curriculum planning—
    Great Britain
    I. Title   II. Ridley, Ken
    372.19′0941   LB1564.G7

ISBN 1—85396—009—8

Typeset by Setrite Typesetter Ltd.
Printed and bound by Athenaeum Press Ltd,
Newcastle upon Tyne

B C D E F G 5 4 3 2 1 0

CONTENTS

ACKNOWLEDGEMENTS

This book owes its inception to the groups of pre-service and in-service students with whom we have worked over several years and whose discussions have generated the topics covered here. Additionally, thanks must be given to Vin Davis for discussions which contributed to Chapter 2 of this book. Acknowledgements are given to the following for permission to reproduce material in this volume: Allen and Unwin for Bruner, J. S. *Beyond the Information Given* and Taylor, J., *Organizing and Integrating the First School Day*; Beckhard, R. for material in Everard, K. B. and Morris, G., *Effective School Management*; Basil Blackwell for Bantock, G. H., *Dilemmas of the Curriculum*; Cassell for Alexander, R., *Primary Teaching* and Meighan, R., *A Sociology of Educating*; Croom Helm and the Open University Press for Harris, A., Lawn, M. and Prescott, W. (eds.), *Curriculum Innovation*; Falmer Press Ltd for Richards, C. (ed.), *New Directions in Primary Education* and Eisner, E., *The Art of Educational Evaluation*; Gower Publishing Group for Oppenheim, A. N., *Questionnaire Design and Attitude Measurement*; Harper and Row Ltd for Everard, K.B. and Morris, G., *Effective School Management* and Skilbeck, M., *School-Based Curriculum Development*; Heinemann Educational Books Ltd for Waters, D., *Primary School Projects*; Heinemann Educational Books Ltd and the Open University Press for McCormick, R. (ed.), *Calling Education to Account*; the Controller of Her Majesty's Stationery Office for *The School Curriculum*; *The Curriculum From 5-16* and *Cmnd. 7212, Special Educational Needs*; Hodder and Stoughton for Horton, T. and Raggart, P. (eds.), *Challenge and Change in the Curriculum*; Lee, V. and Zeldin, D. (eds.), *Planning in the Curriculum* and

Skilbeck, M. (ed.) *Evaluating the Curriculum in the Eighties*; Inner London Education Authority for *The Study of Places in the Primary School*; Kemmis, S. and Taylor and Francis Ltd for *Seven Principles for Programme Evaluation in Curriculum Development and Innovation* (in *Journal of Curriculum Studies*); Lancashire County Council for *Lancashire Looks at...Science in the Primary School*; Lawrence Erlbaum Asociates Ltd (London) for Bennett, N. *et al.*, *The Quality of Pupil Learning Experiences*; Leicester University Press for Galton, M. (ed.), *Curriculum Change: the Lessons of a Decade*; Macmillan (London and Basingstoke) for Clift, P., Weiner, G. and Wilson, E., *Record Keeping in Primary Schools*; Methuen Educational for Stones, E. (ed.) *Readings in Educational Psychology*; Entwistle, H., *Child Centred Education* and Schools Council, *The Practical Curriculum*; Newstead Publishing Educational for Hewlett, M., *Curriculum to Serve Society: How Schools Can Work for People*; NFER–Nelson, Windsor, England, for Dalin, P. and Rust, V. D., *Can Schools Learn?*; The Open University for Ashton, P. *et al.*, *Curriculum in Action: An Approach to Evaluation*; Scrimshaw, P., *Educational Ideologies*; Pluto Press for Wolpe, A. M. and Donald, J. (eds.), *Is There Anyone Here From Education?*; Steward, V. for material in Everard, K. B. and Morris, G., *Effective School Management*; Thames and Hudson Ltd for Flew, A. G. N., *An Introduction to Western Philosophy*; University of London Institute of Education for Hirst, P. (1975) The curriculum and its objectives: a defense of piecemeal rational planning, *The Curriculum: The Doris Lee Lectures (Studies in Education 2)* pp. 14 and 15.

INTRODUCTION

This book has been written in response to several perceived needs among educators both at initial training and in-service levels. From several years of in-service education there has developed in the authors an awareness that serving teachers recognize the need for a theory of the primary curriculum so that they can analyse their own thoughts and practices, heighten their understanding of the settings of, and constraints on, primary curriculum planning, and clarify rationales for curriculum planning. The response of very many teachers to this theoretical overview is notably enthusiastic.

Caught up in the day-to-day world of schooling, the ability to stand back from the classroom is easily diminished, the will to reflect reactively and proactively succumbs to a repetition of successful themes, topics and lessons. A return to theory is both challenging and exciting, offering the means for teachers to meet the problem of selecting relevant experiences for children, to update curricula and to justify their practices. Theoretical study exposes issues which teachers may feel intuitively, which their curriculum planning hints at, but which is seldom fully articulated or examined. In revealing that the curriculum is open, value saturated and negotiable, this is at the same time both threatening and seductive, for while the curriculum is marked by theoretical openness, the practices of many teachers are characterized by theoretical and practical closure.

Perhaps the knowledge that the curriculum could be different is too uncomfortable or unattractive for many teachers; it threatens security and expertise, it offers only the allure of uncertainty. To change the curriculum is destabilizing and deskilling, if not potentially subversive. The attraction of 'altering the system' is parried by the inertia of teachers to curriculum change. Whether or not the study of curriculum theory is sufficient to bring about change is not at issue here; rather the need is for teachers to root their practices in a thought-through view of what constitutes worthwhile experiences, worthwhile learning, worthwhile teaching, worthwhile development, worthwhile progression and worthwhile knowledge. Theory equips teachers in part to approach these problems.

However, theory alone is often unattractive to teachers and students, appearing reified and ill-suited to daily classroom practice. It is seen as a luxury reserved for those unassailed by the need for daily classroom survival. The notion developed in this book runs counter to this; intelligent practice requires information − or intelligence − about the classroom. While such information can be determined by the logic of survival, if teaching and learning have their origin and purpose in the promotion of free thinking then teachers need not abandon the contribution of theory to intelligent behaviour. However, while admitting this, the tenor of this book is towards the 'discovery of grounded theory' (Glaser and Strauss, 1967), an awareness that theory and practice exist symbiotically.

The curriculum planner − at an institutional or individual level − is faced with having to produce a practical outcome at the end of the day − a curriculum. Hence this book seeks to establish practical outcomes of theoretical issues wherever appropriate. This is a dangerous enterprise, for no unitary relationship or set of relationships neither exists nor should exist between theory and practice. Is the task then too invidious, difficult or unacceptable to be attempted? Surely not. If practice is to be informed by theory, and theory by practice, then the enterprise should perhaps be tackled. Hence the translation of theoretical issues into practice and the drawing-upon-practice to advance and illuminate theory is seen as useful and necessary here.

With the intention expressed of developing the theory and practice link in this book, a deliberate attempt has been made to meet the needs of students and teachers in initial appointments and beyond, offering support in the practical management of learning in the primary school. While recognizing the critical role which theory plays in sound classroom practice, clear, usable guidelines for practice are certainly not avoided. These are located in a 'primary ethos' arrived at through an analysis of influences on the curriculum in Chapter 1. Characteristics of the 'primary ethos' are used by curriculum planners as referents in deciding on aims, content, pedagogy, children's experiences, resources and evaluation.

If the spectre of a traditional approach to curriculum planning (a means-end model) appears to haunt this process then this is purely for the purposes of organizing the chapters of the book. In reality the direction of the argument in the book steers away from such a model and towards the notion that planning must be rational − reasoned − and that such reason attaches itself to any and all areas of the curriculum process. To assist planners the notion of applying models as a means of clarifying thinking is discussed in Chapter 2. Similarly, from Chapter 3 onwards each chapter contains a list of questions which can be asked of the content under discussion. This, it is hoped, will enable planners to handle the complexity of the issues in a manageable and systematic form.

There is no single correct way of planning the primary curriculum; there is no simple prescription that can be offered. Rather, this book attempts to offer guidance for planning at several levels − theoretical, managerial, substantive and practical − for the whole school, for groups of teachers or for individuals. The tasks of managing primary curriculum planning, corporately or singly, are addressed by the discussion of issues and outcomes together. They are presented so that teachers and students can grasp the need to link theory and practice, and to interpret the relationship and its outcomes in the primary curriculum. The primary curriculum then is not narrowly conceived of as a prescription for learning activities or content, but as a proposal − to be negotiated, discussed and perhaps changed − about aims, content, organization and structure, management, pedagogy and evaluation. These are all rooted in an analysis of the educational, political, social, philosophical and valuative contexts which influence the practice of education.

1
THEORETICAL CONTEXTS FOR PLANNING THE PRIMARY CURRICULUM

To the school or individual teacher embarking on planning a curriculum a challenging, if not overwhelming, task lies ahead. Teachers have to plan for a diversity of children, organizations and pedagogical principles and practices. How can teachers understand and plan for the world of the primary school, to operate successfully within it? Given that constituents of a 'good' teacher or a 'good' school are dependent on the values of the evaluator, how will success be judged? Notions of 'quality' in teaching and schools are varied, and must be interrogated to expose the value systems which support them. This involves a reflective and critical stance towards teaching; success begins with an understanding of the rationales which comprise primary teaching and then using these to inform planning. Planning thus takes place in accordance with the outcomes of reflection and the development of a questioning attitude to, and critical awareness of, teaching at the stages of planning, implementation and evaluation.

The existence of potential variety in primary teaching should promote a positive attitude and generate an open mind rather than the uniformity of practice which characterizes many primary classrooms (Galton, Simon and Croll, 1980). In this, no one method has universal acceptance or applicability; no simple formula can be provided for successful teaching. Teaching and planning must develop out of a consideration of appropriacy to teachers' personalities, the children in their care, and the types of classroom environments and climates which teachers wish to develop. Enjoyment of teaching and learning rests on the intelligent decisions

1

which teachers are continually having to make. This chapter introduces some conceptual tools for understanding the primary curriculum and the several principles and constraints which have brought it to its present position and which govern its planning.

Primary education and its planning is the product of many trends and influences (Blyth, 1965), some mutually supporting and others conflicting; they are the contexts in which discussions of the primary curriculum are set. An analysis of these contexts − ideological, epistemological, psychological, sociological, managerial and evaluative − paints a composite picture of the primary curriculum as fluid, negotiable, complex and, significantly, changeable; there are very few constants apart from the child and the teacher. Such fluidity and negotiability must be reflected in curriculum planning. A plan becomes a proposal rather than a blueprint or tidy package.

IDEOLOGICAL CONTEXTS

The curriculum is value-based. It is founded on the principle of protection and neglect of selected values. Curriculum planners need to expose such values before evaluating how they are brought into the planning debate. A value or ideology can be defined as 'that system of beliefs which gives general direction to the educational policies of those who hold those beliefs' (Scrimshaw, 1983, p. 4). Different ideologies can coexist with a degree of harmony; different elements of the curriculum being built on different ideological foundations. Alternatively, one can adopt a less consensual line, seeing ideologies not as sets of beliefs of various social groups but − from a Marxian perspective − as that set of values issuing from the dominant powers in society which has imperceptibly permeated the whole class structure; this has the effect of sustaining the dominant class in power (Centre for Contemporary Cultural Studies, 1981).

The significance of this interpretation for curriculum planners is to direct attention to the power of certain groups to make major curriculum decisions, to ask 'whose values are protected in the curriculum?' Educational ideologies will contain values, beliefs and assumptions about children, learning, teaching, knowledge and the curriculum. A curriculum is taken to be all those activities designed or encouraged within the school's organizational framework to promote the intellectual, personal, social and physical development of its pupils. It includes not only the formal programme of lessons, but also the 'informal' programme of so-called extra-curricular activities as well as those features which produce the school's 'ethos'.

More specifically, Meighan (1981) contends than an ideology addresses seven components which concern curriculum planners:

1. A theory of knowledge: its content and structure — what is considered worthwhile or important knowledge, how it is organized (e.g. by subjects or integrated areas) and who shall have access to it.
2. A theory of learning and the learner's role — an active or a passive style, doing or listening, co-operative or competitive learning, producing or reproducing knowledge, problem-solving or receiving facts.
3. A theory of teaching and the teacher's role — formal to informal, authoritarian or democratic, interest in outcomes or processes, narrow or wide.
4. A theory of resources appropriate for learning — first hand or second hand.
5. A theory of organization of learning situations — criteria for grouping pupils.
6. A theory of assessment that learning has taken place — diagnostic or attainment testing, written or observational assessment, defining what is to be assessed.
7. A theory of aims, objectives and outcomes — a view of what is desirable for society, the child, and knowledge.

One can determine how characteristics of different educational ideologies will address these seven main components. Scrimshaw (1983), for example, suggests that ideologies differ in their emphasis on the individual learner, knowledge and society. While these are clearly not discrete, nevertheless the emphasis is useful, and is one way of organizing the potentially disparate number of ideologies which appear in educational literature. Many of these are substantially the same ideology under a different name and are presented in summary form in Table 1.1. The difference between knowledge (a) and knowledge (b) in Table 1.1 lies in the access to high status knowledge. Advocates of knowledge (a) would restrict high status knowledge to an elite minority, whereas advocates of knowledge (b) would make it accessible to all pupils. The difference between society (a) and society (b) lies in the perspectives on society. Society (a) tends to regard the existing societal status quo as desirable and worth perpetuating and improving, while society (b) will look to its alteration, its future evolution.

Ideologies Emphasizing the Individual Learner

Ideologies in this sphere represent the 'developmental tradition' in primary education (Blyth, 1965). In them the transmission of knowledge is sec-

TABLE 1.1 Clusters of educational ideologies

Ideology	Emphasis
Progressivism Child-centredness Romanticism	Individual child
Classical humanism Conservatism Traditionalism Academicism	Knowledge (a)
Liberal humanism	Knowledge (b)
Instrumentalism Revisionism Economic renewal	Society (a)
Democratic socialism Reconstructionism	Society (b)

ondary to discovery and to following the child's impulses, needs and interests. Stress is laid on learning by doing, spontaneity, free expression and developing the child's own nature spontaneously: 'give your scholar no verbal lessons; he should be taught by experience alone' (Worthington, 1884, p. 56). Knowledge is not imposed from without, but is uncertain, pragmatic, tentative and provisional; it is that which the child discovers rather than reproduces.

Emphasis is placed, then, on originality and authenticity of the child's experience and awareness, on diversity of response and provision, on creativity, enjoyment and the development of the emotional side of the child's personality. The process of learning is as important as the outcomes of learning – the knowledge products. Hence education is seen as intrinsically worthwhile; valuable in itself rather than for what it leads to in later life.

In their challenge to rationalism, objectivity, abstract analysis and universalism, these ideologies celebrate empiricism, subjectivity, personal meanings and particularism. Childhood becomes a state in itself rather than a preparation for adulthood: 'the child is the father of the man' (Wordsworth, 1807). Adults can learn from children and their childhood innocence (see also Aries, 1973). For curriculum planners such views refute the value of an imposed curriculum: 'put the problems before him and let him solve them himself...let him not be taught science, let him discover it' (Rousseau, in Blenkin and Kelly, 1981, p. 19).

Schools have to protect children from the harmful and unpleasant aspects of the outside world (King, 1978) which might corrupt them. Hence they cocoon the child in a comfortable and secure environment separate from the vagaries of the world outside the classroom. If children fail at school then the school rather than the child is to be censured. One can detect the inspirational and optimistic rather than the analytic tenor of child-centred ideologies; indeed analysis reveals how dangerously loose these ideologies can be. For example, how can one derive and plan a curriculum from needs and interests which may be trivial, ephemeral, irrelevant or morally unacceptable? How will children judge what their needs are until they have a measure of knowledge? How can a curriculum be constructed from aims such as 'development', 'growth', or 'discovery' (Hirst and Peters, 1970)? Will it not lead to Bantock's (1980, p. 44) fears that 'temporary interest and immediate need are the guiding principle implicit in the attempt to "psychologize" learning; hence the emphasis on motivation and endogenous development too easily fosters a magpie curriculum of bits and pieces'?

Further, in sheltering children from the corruption of the outer world, how adequate an education is being provided for future citizens? How justified is the exclusion or neglect, however partial, of the world beyond the classroom or immediate environment, regardless of the desirability or undesirability of that world? Similarly, in concentrating on the 'here and now' of the child's existence, how fair or responsible are teachers being to the received wisdoms of prior generations? Children may want, and need, to know about conflict and change as well as consensus and stability.

In approaching child-centred ideologies, then, one has to pare away the romanticism and exhortation, address the criticisms, and then see how they can be usefully employed in curriculum planning, avoiding the curriculum myopia to which such ideologies are prone. The thrust of many of these ideologies towards practical discovery and experiential learning, problem-solving, a process approach to the curriculum, identifying, meeting and developing children's needs, abilities and individual personalities, flexibility rather than uniformity of teaching, and the provision of a stimulating environment, become the elements which curriculum planners can use.

Ideologies Emphasizing Knowledge

In these ideologies one can detect a strong sympathy with conservative notions of protecting and perpetuating the best of the past as experienced in the present. Their antecedents lie in the 'preparatory' tradition (Blyth, 1965) of primary education and derive too from Plato's 'Republic' through

Jesuit education, the mandarins of classical Chinese history (Weber, 1972), Matthew Arnold, T. S. Eliot and Bantock. They are unequivocally divisive and elitist, arguing for a separate and elite education into 'high culture' and a high cultural heritage for a chosen minority, giving them access to power and privilege:

> education should help to preserve the class and to select the elite. It is right that the exceptional individual should have the opportunity to elevate himself in the social scale and attain a position in which he can exercise his talents to the greatest benefit of himself and society. But the ideal of an educational system which would automatically sort out everyone according to his native capacities is unattainable in practice.... It would disorganize society, by substituting for classes, elites of brains, or perhaps only of sharp wits.
>
> (Eliot, 1948, pp. 100–1)

Its curriculum is academic and intellectual, nonvocational even though its clients may go on to prestigious positions in employment; it recognizes the permanence of knowledge and of high status knowledge in particular. Children have to be initiated into the received wisdoms of their forbears, the initiation rites of passage often being formal examinations. Subject loyalty is strong, discipline oriented and reliant on instruction rather than experiential learning (Lawton, 1973). Standards are clear, excellence of academic achievement is emphasized, and stress is laid on the development of rationality through a curriculum marked by uniformity rather than diversity (Jenkins, 1975). This curriculum runs counter to social justice and equality of opportunity (Lawton, 1983). For the masses who cannot aspire to this, a 'folk' curriculum (Bantock, 1975;1976) is offered whose result is effectively to debar them from entering the corridors of privilege, providing what is often regarded as low status, practical, vocational and everyday knowledge. Ideologies in this area, then, emphasize a 'dual' curriculum (Scrimshaw, 1976).

Against this perhaps bleak picture an alternative ideology in this area advances a knowledge-based curriculum whose emphasis is less on a stratified than on a unified society, with egalitarian principles at its core. In liberal humanism high culture is to be accessible to all through a common curriculum: 'If, as Tawney said, we think the higher culture fit for solicitors, why should we not think it fit for coalminers?... Every child should be initiated into those forms of experience which together constitute this higher culture – the arts, mathematics, the human and physical sciences, philosophy' (White, 1982b, p. 26). For curriculum planners the significance of debates about knowledge is to clarify which knowledge should be in the curriculum, how it should be organized and who should have access to it.

Ideologies Emphasizing Society

The ideologies in this group share a common belief that education is valued for what it leads to rather than solely being an end in itself. One can discern two clear directions which society-oriented ideologies take. Instrumental ideologies – instrumentalism, revisionism, and those stressing economic renewal – emphasize the need for education to fit learners to society, particularly in economic terms. Education thus exists to provide a skilled workforce to expand the nations's economic strength; hence resources are developed for vocational (Department of Education and Science (DES) 1985c), scientific and technical education. Weight is laid on the relevance and utility aspects of education (Scrimshaw, 1983). The intentions of education are not to alter radically existing society, rather to improve the efficiency of existing organizations, institutions and economic structures (Oliver, 1982).

Contrasted to this are more radical society-oriented educational ideologies. Figuring high at times of social rebuilding or social upheaval, e.g. post-war renewal of society, reconstructionism posits a view of education as a major force for planned change rather than stability in society; what society ought to be rather than what it is (Scrimshaw, 1983). Society in need of reconstruction requires an educated populace whose curriculum has a strong social core with a stress on citizenship, egalitarianism, democracy and participation in decision-making. In this world teachers are catalysts and guardians of social change; creators rather than transmitters of knowledge. There are dangers in this approach. Such a vision is potentially unstable as it is always looking to the future; it is predicated for its success on an educated citizenry – which is perhaps both its greatest strength and its greatest weakness; it relies on a high level of control – running the risk perhaps of centralization or even indoctrination. Finally, one has to question the extent to which education can shoulder the burden of changing society. Do not macro changes require macro and manifold organizations and institutions to change? Reconstructionist ideology, with its positive, perhaps idealistic, tone and central role for education, requires curriculum planners to think from afresh the content, aims and pedagogy of curricula from the perspective of their benefit to society (Hewlett, 1986). From an analysis of key characteristics of different ideologies one can map their expression onto Meighan's (1981) components of ideologies outlined earlier, and they are presented thus in Table 1.2

Ideological analysis affects primary curriculum planning extensively – at the levels of aims, content, pedagogy and evaluation. The analysis so far reveals the multiplicity of values which underpin the curriculum. There is

TABLE 1.2 Ideologies interpreted by their component issues

Ideology	Progressivism, child-centredness, romanticism	Classical humanism, traditionalism, academicism, conservatism	Liberal humanism	Instrumentalism, revisionism, economic renewal	Reconstructionism, democratic socialism
Emphasis	Individual child	Knowledge – unequal access	Knowledge – equal access	Society – status quo	Society – changed.
Theory of knowledge	Empiricist, active, evolutionary, subjective, emphasis on processes, integrated curricula	Disciplines, non-vocational, academic, high culture, emphasis on products, rationalistic	Common culture curriculum	Utilitarian, economically relevant, vocational, scientific, technological	Revolutionary, problem-solving, active, socially relevant, vocational
Theory of learning and of the learner's role	Experiential, spontaneity, emphasis on skills and processes, co-operative, intrinsic motivation	Obedience, passivity, conformity, uniformity	Induction into key areas of experience, active and co-operative learning	Induction into vocationally relevant areas	Apprenticeship, practical, co-operative, problem-solving
Theory of teaching and of the teacher's role	Guide, provider of multiple resources, facilitator, catalyst of child's self-chosen curriculum	Instructor, information transmitter, authoritative, formal tutor	Guide, provider of resources, facilitator	Instructor, trainer, transmitter of vocationally relevant experiences	Guide, catalyst of social changes, disseminator of centralist philosophy, instructor, trainer
Theory of resources	First-hand, diverse, extensive	Second-hand, restricted	First and second hand, multiple, extensive	Narrowly relevant to content, practical, vocational	Highly focused to task in hand, vocational

Theory of organisation of learning situations	Diverse, flexible, informal, co-operative, group work, discovery methods	Class teaching, formal, uniform, competitive	Open, flexible, diverse	Narrow, practical, relevant to task, class and individual teaching, uniformity	Individual and group work as relevant to task
Theory of assessment	Diagnostic, multiple criteria, informal, profiling	Written, formal, attainment testing, examinations	Diagnostic, norm and written, formal or informal	Formal, written and oral, practical	Flexible, formal or written as appropriate, attainment testing
Theory of aims, objectives and outcomes	Self-expression, individuality, creativity, development of whole personality	Received curricula, elitist, non-vocational, high culture	Equal access to key areas of knowledge, egalitarian	Extrinsic worthwhileness, relevant to economic good, efficient worker	Extrinsic worthwhileness, relevant to social good, citizenship, common good

no exclusive relationship between the ideologies and the everyday activities of primary schools; the same activity in school can support a variety of ideologies, just as one ideology can give rise to several activities. Further, different areas of the curriculum can, and will, serve different educational ideologies. The effect of this analysis is twofold: first, it reveals, importantly, that the curriculum is not a closed system, but that it is open, negotiable, problematic, and has to be constantly reviewed, questioned and discussed. Second, ideological analysis reveals potential conflicts in curriculum decision-making. If one queries why certain ideologies are over-represented or under-represented in the primary curriculum, one is thrust back on to an examination of the power structures operating in curriculum decision-making, to identify whose decisions are holding sway. As mentioned earlier, ideological investigation can reveal the nature of the power of dominant interest groups; ideological analysis is thus political analysis (Mannheim, 1936).

Schools and teachers are caught up in this, like it or not. The study of ideologies, while it separates artificially practices in the interests of conceptual clarity, assists teachers and planners to adopt the reflective and critical stance advocated at the outset of this chapter as a requisite of 'good' teaching. Curriculum planners will need to ascertain the power behind curriculum proposals emanating from diverse sources.

EPISTEMOLOGICAL CONTEXTS

While ideological contexts of the curriculum are fundamental to an understanding of primary practice, they are allied clearly to epistemological contexts — concerns with knowledge, its forms and structures. One can approach this area by posing the question 'what do we mean by knowing?' — a central question for curriculum planning. From Ryle (1949) can be taken two familiar terms to describe knowing: 'knowing that' and 'knowing how'. 'Knowing that' is concerned with what can be stated in propositions and facts, e.g. I know *that* the Prime Minister lives at 10, Downing Street; I know *that* this fridge is broken. Much educational knowledge is necessarily of this type. The weakness of 'knowing that' is its lack of utility: we may know the theory of something, e.g. driving, and yet be unable to drive in practice. Similarly, we may know the practice of something, e.g. that a fridge works, but not know why or how. What is required is Ryle's second type of knowledge, 'knowing how': understanding, possessing 'skills, techniques, trained capacities to perform in practical situations where pupils' expressive capacities are relevant and useful' (Skilbeck and Harris, 1976, p. 67). 'Knowing how' is the ability to do things well or correctly, e.g. to drive, to ride a bicycle. The implications of this for curriculum planners are twofold. First, we need to redress the balance in education, which presently over-represents 'knowing that' – inert ideas (Whitehead, 1932) – in favour of a greater emphasis on 'knowing how' – processes. Second, we can learn about things – 'knowing that' – by adopting appropriate processes – 'knowing how'. For example, children can learn the value of co-operation by behaving co-operatively; perhaps through group work, they can learn about music by playing or writing it. In similar vein, Smith (1971) contends that the best way for children to learn about reading is by actually reading. Ideas and concepts are used actively rather than aggregated and stored.

A second key epistemological dichotomy in primary education contends that knowledge is reached through reason, thought and reflection, independent of the senses – which are notoriously fallible. A central area of rationalist enquiry is mathematics. For example, if we ask 'How do you know that 91 minus 36 equals 55?' it is inappropriate to reply 'I looked at it and saw it', but 'I figured it out'. One resorts to calculation, not seeing or hearing; one reasons it out. As Flew (1971) comments: 'propositions of this kind are discoverable by the mere operation of thought, without dependence on what is anywhere existent in the universe. Though there never was a circle or triangle in nature, the truths demonstrated by Euclid would forever retain their certainty and evidence' (p. 384).

In rationalism knowledge is independent of the observer. It claims to provide universal truths; the development of rationality thus becomes a central educational aim. With its emphasis on logic and reason, rationalism appeals strongly to mathematics and to the spheres of values, aims and morals, where reasoning might be a better way of investigating the issues rather than relying on observed experience. However, the main thrust of rationalism for curriculum planners is to argue for the unchallengeable right of some subjects to be included in the curriculum – either because they develop rationality or because they are intrinsically and objectively worthwhile.

Subjects are included in the curriculum because they have objective value regardless of human perception. The problem with this is that while it may suggest the inclusion of mathematics or morality in the curriculum or require curriculum planners to address the problem of how to develop rationality in children, it is difficult to see how using the rationalist argument can in practice offer guidelines or guidance on what to select for the curriculum. At a philosophical level, objective intrinsic worthwhileness is impossible to demonstrate; conceptions of rationality, rational thought and behaviour differ; they are context-dependent. It is difficult therefore to argue the rights of any subject to be included in the curriculum by appealing to universal truths (Blenkin and Kelly, 1981).

While rationality might be one way of achieving knowledge, there are some types of knowledge which are not available through rationality alone — sensory knowledge. Empiricism is premissed on the notion that knowledge is only acquired through sensory experience and reflection on perceptions. For the empiricist, knowledge must correspond to the observed facts of the case. If one accepts the empiricist view then there are five main implications for primary curriculum planners. Initially the objectivity or universal validity of knowledge is replaced by a version of knowledge which sees it as unique, tied to specific contexts; a far more tentative, hypothetical and evolutionary version. Knowledge is subject to constant modification and obsolescence. This is perhaps a more accurate picture of the contemporary knowledge and information explosion than rationalism would offer. Second, knowledge becomes equated with experiences; the direct and first-hand experiences of the child are central to any educational endeavour. Third, teaching styles will have to be revised to reflect the tentative view of knowledge, to resist the imposition of knowledge in favour of the creation and discovery of knowledge — a more problem-solving, discovery approach.

If truth or knowledge are uncertain, temporary and provisional, any attempt by teachers to impose such knowledge on children must be suspect and unsatisfactory, since it is likely to inhibit rather than to promote the continuing evolution of knowledge by offering it in a form that suggests it is fixed and static rather than revealing the fluid entity it really is (Blenkin and Kelly, 1981).

Fourth, teaching will have to move to a process rather than a product view of knowledge, concentrating on skills of knowledge-getting rather than outcomes, e.g. enquiry skills and evaluation skills. Knowledge is to be tested rather than passively accepted (Bruner, 1970). Hence children will be working, for example, as a historian works. Rather than simply learning facts and dates, they will be working in the scientific method of formulating and testing hypotheses, controlling variables and carefully observing results rather than solely reciting scientific facts and concepts. Fifth, empiricism renders selection and curriculum planning problematic as it runs the risk of an imposed curriculum which may not fairly reflect the tentative view of knowledge (Alexander, 1984). Therefore, curriculum planners may need to temper the excitement of empiricism with the demands of coping and survival strategies.

In planning for the primary curriculum, the further epistemological questions which are raised concern how knowledge is to be structured and organized and whether it is to be organized on subject or integrated lines. The arguments about the benefits of one or the other conceal the conceptual confusion surrounding both terms. Subjects can derive from the disciplines of knowledge, with their own central concepts, modes of enquiry, distinctive logical structures and truth tests. Such disciplines could be articulated thus (Hirst, 1965):

mathematical knowledge
physical sciences
human sciences
history
religion
literature and fine arts
philosophy

However, the number and constitution of the disciplines is a major problematic area in epistemology. For example, Peterson (1975) gives four − logical, empirical, moral, aesthetic − while Schwab (1975) gives three − investigative disciplines (mathematics and natural sciences), appreciative disciplines (arts) and decisive disciplines (social sciences). Phenix (1975) gives six:

symbolics (languages, mathematics, logic)
empirics (physical and social sciences)
esthetics (arts)
synnoetics (relational insight, interpersonal awareness)
ethics (morals)
synoptics (history, religion and philosophy)

To say, then, that subjects should represent the disciplines is therefore to invite potential confusion into planning. Alternatively, subjects can be interdisciplinary − e.g. geography, home economics, human and social studies (DES, 1985a, 1985b) − where they integrate knowledge from the disciplines into topics and themes (houses, farms, water) − the stuff of the primary curriculum. Thus there is a lack of clarity on the term 'subject' (Peters, 1969). If the notion of a 'subject' is ambiguous then it is equally so for the notion of 'integrated' knowledge. What is being integrated: is it the disciplines of knowledge or the children's experiences? If it is the former then the question must be raised of the extent to which teachers can successfully integrate knowledge which by its disciplinary pedigree cannot fairly be integrated; if it is the latter then one has to ask how teachers can ensure that children understand the integration and the integrating principle (Taba, 1962). For many children the integrated curriculum is incoherent, a random assortment of loosely connected or disconnected facts and activities.

Given this clouded starting point, primary teaching, devolved both on subject and on integrated lines, stems from different epistemological parentage. For subject teaching the arguments arrange themselves around the notions of quality, excellence, tradition, high standards, high culture, sensitivity to ways of meeting and developing curricula from an analysis of children's needs through informed knowledge. Against this it is argued that subjects preserve outworn traditional knowledge, that they fragment a child's experience, that they are representative of a concern more with knowledge than the learner; a measure of inflexibility in content and pedagogy. In short, they embody the conservative ideologies outlined earlier. On the other hand, integrated knowledge serves the child-centred ideologies which emphasize the whole child, unity of experience, and the need to develop both the cognitive and the affective sides of the child's personality. There is a direct line which can be drawn between 'preparatory' histories, conservative ideologies, rationalist epistemologies and subject teaching on one side, and 'developmental' histories, child-centred ideologies, empiricist epistemologies and integrated types of knowledge on the other (c.f. Alexander, 1984). Dependent on one's value position will be the emphasis given to either strand in the planning of curricula.

It is possible then to reaffirm the conclusion reached at the end of the ideological discussion, that the curriculum of the primary school is not predicated on a single set of values. It is epistemologically value saturated, and as such it is open, tentative and negotiable. Different areas of the curriculum are premissed on different epistemologies. Epistemological analysis clarifies the problematic nature of selecting content, although it does not, nor cannot, answer the questions which it raises. That is a matter for personal or collective debate, reflection and open-minded discussion — the hallmarks of high quality planning.

PSYCHOLOGICAL CONTEXTS

Curriculum planners need to have a clear understanding of how learning takes place and how it can best be promoted through teaching and learning styles. Such an understanding derives from psychological theory. The foci of such theory comprehend:

1. The nature of the learner
   (a) cognitive and affective aspects
   (b) individual differences
   (c) individual needs
2. The nature of the learning process
   (a) learning theories

(b) motivation – extrinsic and intrinsic
(c) active learning
(d) reinforcement and feedback
(e) readiness and matching
(f) measurement and diagnosis
(g) structuring and sequencing learning
(h) transfer of learning skills
(i) role of language
(j) nature of child development

Behaviourist Theories

In these importance is attached to a very precise analysis and sequencing of what is to be learned, step-by-step learning, with each new learning being rewarded or reinforced. Learning is evidenced by observable changes in behaviour; the desired learning objective is broken down into the steps or processes which lead to the achievement of that objective. The influence of this type of approach can be seen generally in the ways in which teachers sequence and reinforce the learning of desired objectives and skills, and in particular examples such as reading workshops, SRA laboratories, and reading and mathematics schemes which operate through a carefully controlled sequence of new material.

However, behaviourist theories have been castigated for several reasons. They cast the learner in a very passive role: children are receivers of programmes (Taylor, 1968) or predetermined sequences whereas 'the individual is best viewed neither as a passive recipient of information nor as a bundle of stimulus–response connections. Rather he should be regarded as an active participant in the knowledge-getting process' (Bruner, 1974, p. 397). It is difficult to see how programmed learning can develop critical awareness and independent thought in children – an increasingly significant feature in a plural society marked by controversy and conflict (Ing, 1981), and a central feature of the primary ethos. Moreover, it is hard to imagine just how workable the idea is that complex and abstract concepts can be broken down into sequential steps; either the number of steps is unmanageably long, or the steps are poorly sequenced, or, more damaging still, it risks having only trivial or low-level objectives addressed – the same argument that has been levelled at behavioural objectives (MacDonald-Ross, 1975). Like the problems of behavioural objectives, the behavioural theories of psychology confuse logical steps with psychological steps (Hirst, 1967).

They imply only one pathway through knowledge and a didactic and prescriptive teaching style. They equate a classroom with a clinical laboratory, unsullied by the realities of primary schools (c.f. Pollard, 1985).

Cognitive Theories

There are two key figures in this discussion, Piaget and Bruner. From Piaget can be taken the notion that learning is an active process through manipulating actual experiences (Kamii, 1975). For Piaget, learning is achieved through a process of assimilation and accommodation of experiences. He lays stress on the importance of social relationships — peer-group teaching and group work — as one important way of breaking free from the egocentricity characteristic of young children. Piaget both contributes to epistemological theory and fuels child-centred ideologies, for in his theories of cognitive development, from sensori-motor to formal operations, children change their thinking qualitatively as they grow.

The ideological impact of this qualitative difference in thinking between children and adults is to argue that children have status as children rather than solely as miniature or future adults. Their needs as children must be met, differences must be respected. Piaget's 'stages' theory also lends itself to introducing the concept of matching (discussed later) and readiness; that one can match a child's work if one knows which stage of development she or he has reached or is ready to meet. The concept of matching has urgency if one considers the overwhelming evidence of poor matching found by Bennett, Desforges and Wilkinson (1984), where 54 per cent of number tasks and 55 per cent of language tasks were mismatched.

However, Piaget's work must be treated with caution (Donaldson, 1978). Nisbet (1983) regards the stage theory of development with suspicion, lest it become too narrowly prescriptive — 'a disguised version of behaviouristic determination' (p. 83), trapping children's development by planning work for stages which they may have left in many conceptual areas (see also Alexander, 1984).

Like Piaget, Bruner argues for the centrality of the child constructing her or his own knowledge rather than receiving it from outside; learning is by active discovery. Epistemologically, this lays great store on process and empiricist views of knowledge, views embodied in his MACOS project (Jenkins, 1976), where emphasis is laid on enquiry, observation, judgement, evaluation and reflection. Knowledge is speculative, therefore what pupils derive from the material cannot be determined completely in advance (Kelly, 1980). Bruner develops a theory of instruction (1966; 1970) which, he claims, has four main features:

1. It should provide experiences which stimulate curiosity in children – a 'predisposition to learning'.
2. It should structure knowledge in a way which can be readily assimilated by children. Structures of knowledge may be learned, he suggests, in three main ways: the enactive mode (knowing something through doing it); the iconic mode (knowing something through seeing or constructing a picture or image of it); and the symbolic mode (knowing something through symbolic means, e.g. language).
3. It 'should specify the most effective sequences in which to present the materials to be learned' (Bruner, 1970, p. 113); this must have due regard to the need to match the logical aspects of a subject to the learner's strategies of learning. Bruner, like Hirst (1967), insists that there is no single sequence of learning; learning depends for example on an individual's speed of learning, motivation, stage of development, previous knowledge and mode of learning.
4. It 'should specify the nature and pacing of rewards and punishments in the process of learning and teaching' (p. 114). Clearly, Bruner is alluding to the need for careful use of intrinsic and extrinsic motivation, a diagnostic approach to identifying children's needs, and the need to provide positive feedback to children.

In regard to the contribution of these theories to curriculum planning, it can be seen that behaviourist theories lend themselves to training and instruction in a narrow sense of specific and measurable skills – a limited conception of education – whereas alternative theories seem more open-ended. Psychological theories underline the central need to diagnose, evaluate and meet children's needs and abilities; to utilize and generate motivation in children; to offer appropriate rewards and punishments; to cast learning in an active, experiential, discovery mode (DES 1985b); to make learning meaningful (c.f. Smith, 1978); to offer feedback to children; to develop and operate from a positive self-concept in children; to plan on the 'moderate novelty principle' – making tasks and reasons for them explicit and challenging and yet not too remote (Siann and Ugwuegbu, 1980); to accept that there is a place, albeit limited, for rote learning to make responses automatic.

There is an important connection between cognitive psychologies, child-centred and progressive ideologies and empiricist epistemologies. However, attention must be drawn to the very generalized nature of the psychological theories outlined, to question whether they offer teachers little more than platitudes. The theories appear so diffuse as to be able to underscore a variety of conflicting practices. They require reflection and application for their substance. They are not hard and fast truths; they are conflicting, provisional, incomplete and falsifiable. The ramifications of this are once again to suggest that the curriculum and its planning are open to debate, problematic and negotiable.

SOCIOLOGICAL CONTEXTS

The curriculum of a school fulfils social functions; it responds to social requirements and pressures for change. Thus curriculum planning must look to characteristics and constraints of society to find purpose and direction.

The advent of the micro-chip has accelerated the information revolution and the information-based society. Knowledge is expanding at an exponential rate, a move matched by its rate of obsolescence. Schools and society have to develop mechanisms to tolerate such movements. Further, much of this knowledge and its application points towards an increasingly technological mode of operation. The ramifications of this are huge. One major implication is that traditional skills, practices and values are rendered obsolete (Sivanandan, 1979, Stonier, 1982). Society is being compelled to revise its notions of leisure and employment; leisure appears to be a growth area while employment both fluctuates and changes its patterns. The moral problems are vast. Whether to move to full employment or unemployment where technology both deskills and has the potential to reduce the size of the workforce required, is as much a moral question as it is political, economic or technical (Entwistle, 1981).

Second, with knowledge expanding in all directions, increased specialization and fragmentation of interests is inevitable. The central unifying spine of society is ever more difficult to identify; plural values, plural cultures, lifestyles, economics, politics – all are hallmarks of a society marked by a slender reduction in inequality (Westergaard and Resler, 1976), an increased materialism (Apple, 1982) and a loss of social cohesion. Further, the signs of societal strain are clear – urban and industrial decline, rising crime, juvenile delinquency, riots on city streets, and a widening gap between rich and poor. Pluralism is spilling over into conflict. The implications of this again are to reassert the necessity for examining moral problems and values. Technology, with its capability and capacity to create and destroy life in ways scarcely envisaged a generation ago, throws into sharper relief pressing moral problems – abortion, war, health, pollution, poverty. Morality must not be the casualty of technological advance. Further, the extent to which fragmentation of interests can be tolerated needs to be examined.

The educational implications of this scenario are vast. Given that the curriculum at its best can only be a selection from the culture then the criteria for that selection are problematic. To what extent can diverse and conflicting values in society be represented in the curriculum? Whose values are protected in the curriculum, whose neglected? Is the move to a common national curriculum an attempt to retrieve social consensus and cohesion? What will be the nature of the schools' responses to a technologically advancing society? How far can schools act as agents of social change? How far can one look to schools to shoulder the burden of macro-sociological problems?

Curriculum planners can address these issues on many fronts. First, curricula need to represent diverse values and cultures in society — multi-ethnically and subculturally. This raises questions of the extent to which individual schools and communities can determine their own curricula, and the extent to which all schools should be developing in children an awareness of the multiplicity of cultures in society and the problems and possibilities that this offers. Second, at a major decision-making level, there is the need to address the notion of a common curriculum, its desirability, feasibility and practicability, composition and framing — be it through subjects, areas of experience, themes, learning experiences or learning environments (Curriculum Development Centre (CDC), 1980). Third, there is a clear requirement for schools to enable moral debate to take place, to deal with moral issues explicitly as well as implicitly and opportunistically (Lawton, 1983). Fourth, schools must ensure that children have an understanding of political, social and economic systems and power structures in society (ibid, Harwood, 1985).

Fifth, the whole relationship of education and employment requires exploration and rationalization. Such a relationship is tension ridden, for while education celebrates developing individual potential and diversity, the exact opposite is true for vast areas of employment, where a narrow application of skills is practised and where individuality and personal development do not even enter the calculus. Schools make far greater demands on children, and have the potential for offering them richer personal rewards, than does working life. This is not to neglect the significant role that schools must play in teaching numeracy and literacy, indeed, with the rise of the service sector this becomes more pressing. Sixth, just as there is the need to re-examine the relationship between school and work, so there is between education and leisure (Entwistle, 1981). Seventh, the whole nature of technological education needs to be examined to allow for developing in children both a general and specific understanding of technology and its social implications and applications (Lawton, 1983). Eighth, to be able to cope with the knowledge explosion and the rate of obsolescence of knowledge there is a need, recognized by

Her Majesty's Inspectorate (HMI) (DES, 1985b) to teach children skills of information handling, studying, problem-solving and communication (Lawton, 1983). The move to skills-based teaching, though significant, cannot be done in a knowledge vacuum; rather the whole area of content selection becomes problematic. Finally, the effects of change in technology, employment patterns and prospects, information processing, social diversity and cultural pluralism are to put a premium on developing personal and social skills in children (DES, 1981) – adaptability, self-reliance, self-development, personal and environmental responsibility. Planning for the curriculum to promote personal development requires careful consideration of the positive value of child-centredness as an enabling curriculum for developing autonomy in children.

The implications of an analysis of broad societal trends reveal the problematic nature of the primary curriculum. If society is changing, fragmenting and unsure of its directions or its areas of commonality, then the same may be reflected in the primary curriculum. Aims, content, pedagogy, criteria for evaluation are uncertain. A curriculum rests on shifting grounds, yet it must set a firm foundation from reflective, articulate and insightful planners.

The analysis so far is presented in summary form in Table 1.3. The primary curriculum is, and should be, negotiable. Given the inability to offer a single and enduring conceptualization of the primary curriculum, any approaches to planning will inevitably be value saturated. However, they should fairly address the conceptual analysis presented earlier by:

1. Reflecting the negotiable character of the primary curriculum.
2. Addressing macro constraints on the primary curriculum and teachers.
3. Analysing ways in which the primary curriculum is developing.
4. Anticipating, preparing for and serving changes at a macro-societal level.

TABLE 1.3   Ideologies and their background contexts

	Instrumentalism	Conservatism	Progressivism
Focus of the ideology	Society	Knowledge	Child
Emphasis of the curriculum	Efficiency, usefulness, vocationalism, science and technology	Homogeneity, uniformity	Discovery, activity, diversity, needs and interests
	Common curricula	Dual curricula	Diverse curricula

TABLE 1.3   (cont'd)

	Instrumentalism	Conservatism	Progressivism
View of the child	Child as embryonic adult	Child as deficient adult	Childhood as a state in itself
View of knowledge	Societally determined Socially relevant Vocational, useful Empiricist Evolutionary Product and process Extrinsically worthwhile Trained Egalitarian Structured	Unchanging Received, vicarious Non-vocational Rationalist Closed Product Intrinsically worthwhile Initiated Elitist Subject-based	Evolutionary, obsolescent Reflexive, first-hand Non-vocational Empiricist Open-ended, discovered Process Intrinsically worthwhile Discovered, experienced Individual Integrated
Psychologial implications	Behaviourist Understanding Group and individual learning Extrinsic motivation Need for sequence Task-centred learning Programmed learning	Behaviourist and Brunerian Acceptance Class learning Extrinsic motivation Need for structure Competition Structured learning	Developmental and Piagetian Meaningfulness, discovered Flexible learning organizations Intrinsic motivation Need for diversity Co-operation Autonomous learning
Roles of teacher	Trainer, instructor, director	Expert, authority, director	Guide, facilitator catalyst
Roles of child	Apprentice	Neophyte	Agent of own learning
Sociological implications	Education for leisure, social sciences curriculum, multicultural and technological education	Curriculum change from within, seeking equilibrium	Development of creativity, autonomy, self-reliance, adaptability, skills-based teaching

5. Being able to be translated into practice by curriculum planners.
6. Assisting teachers and planners to become critical and reflective in a desire to promote and perpetuate high-quality teaching.

In reviewing the discussions and issues presented so far a checklist of principles can be devised which, taken together, can be said to constitute the 'primary ethos' (Morrison, 1986b):

1. A view of childhood as a state in itself as well as a preparation for adulthood.
2. The use of discovery methods and practical activity.
3. Learning by doing − practical activity.
4. Problem-solving approaches to teaching and learning.
5. Learning in various modes; enactive, iconic, symbolic.
6. Integration and unity of experiences; the integrated curriculum.
7. The value of teaching processes and skills as well as products and bodies of knowledge.
8. A view of content and process as complementary facets of curricular knowledge.
9. A view of educational activities and processes as being intrinsically worthwhile as well as having instrumental and utility value.
10. The value of an enriching social, emotional and physical environment.
11. The need to develop autonomy in children.
12. The provision of a curriculum which demonstrates and allows for breadth, balance, relevance, continuity and progression, differentiation and consistency.
13. The emphasis given to individual needs, abilities, interests, learning styles and rates as well as a received curriculum.
14. The fostering and satisfaction of curiosity.
15. The value of peer group support.
16. The value of self-expression.
17. The need for intrinsic as well as extrinsic motivation.
18. The use of the environment to promote learning.
19. The importance of the quality and intensity of a child's experience.
20. The uniqueness of each child.
21. The view of the teacher as a catalyst for all forms of development.
22. An extended view of the 'basics' to comprehend all curriculum areas, not just the three Rs.
23. The need to develop literacy and numeracy through cross-curricular approaches.

Such a checklist endeavours to meet two demands outlined at the start of this book: the need to provide principles which underpin planning, and, in recognition of the desirability of open-ended, divergent perspectives on primary teaching, the need to offer substance for reflective thinking and debate by teachers.

MANAGEMENT CONTEXTS

Between the theoretical contexts outlined so far and the practical day-to-day planning and implementation of the primary curriculum is set the interface of the management of the curriculum. This can be defined as the most effective use and organization of a spectrum of resources to enable children's learning to be at its optimal level, from planning to implementation, outcomes, evaluation and curriculum change and development (c.f. Bush, 1986). The management of primary school curriculum planning will seek to find major ways of translating the theoretical constructs and constituents of the primary ethos outlined earlier into curricula which are worthwhile and effective. Hence the analysis presented so far has to be taken to substantive levels, to deal with the issues involved in managing the curriculum. This involves addressing three key questions:

1. What are the levels of curriculum management?
2. What are the tasks of curriculum management?
3. What are the styles of curriculum management?

The Tasks in Curriculum Management

The case has been put for regarding the primary curriculum as a negotiation, discussion or exploration of proposals for what teachers should teach and for what children should learn, based on participants' ideologies, epistemologies, views of learning and views of society. Hence the management of the curriculum will involve debate and decision-making on three factors (Day, Johnston and Whitaker, 1985):

1. The planning, philosophies and policies of the curriculum.
2. The operation of the curriculum.
3. The evaluation of the curriculum.

However, the debate does not rest there, for one can suggest that, because the curriculum is about people interacting in a given setting, and because the curriculum is open to debate, managing the curriculum should involve: managing people; managing organizations; and managing change. (Everard and Morris, 1985).

Managing people

Managing people will involve utilizing and developing their interpersonal skills and sensitivities, leadership capabilities, expertise in curriculum areas, interests and aptitudes, enthusiasm and motivation, effort, decision-making capacities, and their abilities to identify and handle conflict (Morrison, 1986a). Managing organizations from a curriculum perspective rather than a routinely administrative perspective involves: the development, effective and appropriate use of team work (Bush, 1986); shared decision-making; open communication channels (vertical and lateral); dissemination channels for new ideas; clarity of aims, philosophies and powers; stable organizational structures in which people can operate; available resources of time, money, space and administration — the technology to support the meeting of the organization's goals (Elliott-Kemp and Williams, 1979); co-ordination of activities; and co-ordinated use of staff expertise.

Managing organizations

Managing people, an idiographic, individualized concern, clearly relies on effectively managing organizations and vice versa. A path has to be set which reconciles and manages several key tensions (Dalin and Rust, 1983):

> Consensus versus conflict;
> Re-stabilization versus renewal of the curriculum;
> The individual versus the organization;
> Leadership versus the staff;
> Process of planning and change versus the content of planning and change;
> Shared ownership of the curriculum versus self-interest of individuals in the curriculum.

Managing change

Both managing people and organizations are synthesized in the notion of managing curriculum change and development. Curriculum innovation, development and change can be articulated as a multifaceted phenomenon (Dalin, 1978), involving regarding it as:

1. An evolutionary process over time rather than as a single event – from invention through development, dissemination and diffusion, to adoption, implementation, institutionalization and recommendation (Hall, Loucks, Rutherford *et al.*, 1975).
2. System disturbing; changes in one area of a school's organization and curriculum setting off a chain reaction in other areas, i.e. that it affects a system rather than a single teacher or instance.
3. A multi-dimensional phenomenon; political, social, organizational, individual, technical.
4. A series of transformations of ideas into practices, institutions and materials.
5. Involving all members of an institution and the complex interplay between individuals and organizational structures.
6. Having to address the rate, staging, scale, degree and continuity of the process (Hoyle, 1976).

The complexity of change and innovation can be realized in answers to the questions:

- Innovations for whom? (Not everyone might benefit from the change; one person's benefit is another's loss in curriculum management.)
- Innovations by whom? (Who has the power, legitimacy and credibility to initiate, implement and support change?)
- Who has to change? (Changes can upset power hierarchies.)
- What has to change? (A school's aims and philosophies, organizations and administration, roles and role relationships, curriculum aims, content, pedagogy, resources, evaluation.)

These many facets all point to the need for management of curriculum change to address the institution in which the change and development is taking place as well as the curriculum itself. This involves addressing the climate (Halpin, 1966) or 'organizational health' (Miles, 1965) of the institution; an institution which is unhealthy is unprepared for curriculum change and development. A school staff or any part of it wishing to innovate a piece of the curriculum may well have to set its institutional health in order before it can innovate in the curriculum; its health must be robust. Hoyle (1975a) reinforces this point where he comments that 'curriculum innovation requires change in the internal organization of the school. Change in the internal organization of the school is a major innovation' (p. 332).

An organizationally healthy school (Miles, 1965) will be clear on its goals, have adequate channels of communication, adequate resources of time, space, money, administrative services, staff (Fullan, 1982), comprise a cohesive staff, tolerate and resolve dissension, encourage teamwork, be able to identify problems, match leadership by the head with leadership by staff, involve staff in curriculum development and discussion, share affective and social relationships as well as institutional relationships, maintain high morale, respect teacher autonomy, foster creativity, be open to self-criticism, operate staff development and INSET plans, and be open to innovation − the list becomes endless!

Collegial decision-making

The model, then, is of 'collegial' rather than 'hierarchical' decision-making (Campbell, 1985). To achieve this may mean overcoming differences of value or power, separately or in combination, tackling barriers to innovation: increased workloads, deskilling which innovation brings (MacDonald, 1975), inappropriate organizational arrangements, lack of resources, edging staff out of a natural reluctance to change, lack of capability to perform new roles (Gross, Giacquinta and Bernstein, 1971), to see change as a benefit, as unthreatening, as evolving from existing practice, as supported by many parties, as a means of increasing job satisfaction and professional development.

Thus a manager of change has to possess several qualities which can be said to lie in the fields of knowledge, skills and personality. This involves addressing the questions set out in Tables 1.4, 1.5, and 1.6. Stewart (1985) highlights characteristics of good managers in Table 1.7. A school which is seeking to improve its organizational development (Dalin and Rust, 1983) can utilize a variety of strategies:

1. Training or education, including lectures, exercises, simulations.
2. Process consultation, concentration on observing ongoing processes and providing feedback.
3. Confrontation, bringing together units or groups which have a history of poor communication.
4. Data feedback, involving systematic collection of information which is reported back to the organization.
5. Plan-making, dealing with planning and goal-setting.
6. Organizational development task force establishment, setting up *ad hoc* groups to provide structure for solving problems and carrying out plans.
7. Techno-structure activity, focusing on structural factors, work flow and means of accomplishing tasks (Schmuck and Miles, 1983).

TABLE 1.4   Knowledge required for managing change

Knowledge of:
1. People and their motivational systems − what makes them tick
2. Organizations as social systems − what makes them healthy and effective, able to achieve objectives
3. The environment surrounding the organization − the systems that impinge on and make demands of it
4. Managerial styles and their effects on work
5. One's own personal managerial style and proclivities
6. Organizational processes such as decision-making, planning, control, communication, conflict management and reward systems
7. The process of change
8. Educational and training methods and theory

(Source: Everard and Morris (1985) *Effective School Management*, p. 180)

TABLE 1.5   Skills required for managing change

Skills in:
1. Analysing large complex systems
2. Collecting and processing large amounts of information and simplifying it for action
3. Goal-setting and planning
4. Getting consensus decisions
5. Conflict management
6. Empathy
7. Political behaviour
8. Public relations
9. Consulting and counselling
10. Training and teaching

(Source: Everard and Morris (1985) *Effective School Management*, p. 181)

TABLE 1.6   Personality characteristics required for managing change

1. A strong sense of personal ethics which helps to ensure consistent behaviour
2. Something of an intellectual by both training and temperament
3. A strong penchant towards optimism
4. Enjoyment of the intrinsic rewards of effectiveness, without the need for public approval
5. High willingness to take calculated risks and live with the consequences without experiencing undue stress
6. A capacity to accept conflict and enjoyment in managing it
7. A soft voice and low-key manner
8. A high degree of self-awareness − knowledge of self
9. A high tolerance of ambiguity and complexity
10. A tendency to avoid polarizing issues into black and white, right and wrong
11. High ability to listen

(Source: Everard and Morris (1985) *Effective School Management*, p. 181)

TABLE 1.7   Characteristics of good managers of change

1. They know clearly what they want to achieve
2. They can translate desires into practical action
3. They can see proposed changes not only from their own viewpoint but also from that of others
4. They do not mind being out on a limb
5. They show irreverance for tradition but respect for experience
6. They plan flexibly, matching constancy of ends against a repertoire of available means
7. They are not discouraged by setbacks
8. They harness circumstances to enable change to be implemented
9. They clearly explain change
10. They involve their staff in the management of change and protect their security
11. They don't pile one change on top of another, but await assimilation
12. They present change as a rational action
13. They make change personally rewarding for people, wherever possible
14. They share maximum information about possible outcomes
15. They show that change is 'related to the business'
16. They have a history of successful change behind them

(Source: Stewart, in Everard and Morris (1985) *Effective School Management*. pp. 179–180)

Dalin and Rust (1983) stress the need for internal and external support for change to be provided to motivate, sustain and shape the direction of the change (c.f. Lavelle, 1984).

It is clear that such skills draw on an ability to state goals, to plan, organize, control, lead and direct people and projects (Everard and Morris, 1985). How this is done can be termed the 'style of curriculum management'.

Styles of Curriculum Management

These concern all parties in the planning process, and depend on the climate of the school and the nature of curriculum leadership in it. For instance, curriculum planners may adopt any of four styles (Loubser, Spiers and Moody, 1975; Tannenbaum and Schmidt, 1985):

1. Tell decisions – autocratic.
2. Sell decisions – paternalistic.
3. Consult decisions – consultative.
4. Share decisions – democratic.

The need to achieve both successful results and successful relationships will guide the selection of styles. There is a trade-off between the styles, whichever are chosen. For example a 'tell' decision can effect a bureaucratic, hierarchical model of planning which reinforces zones of power and influence. While this may be necessary, desirable or expedient, it risks alienating those who receive the decisions. 'Sell' decisions may suit a leader who wishes to foster friendly relations and yet maintain a firm rein on curricular practices; in fact, the opposite may result, the recipients seeing the style as non-genuine (Halpin, 1966), over-assertive, non-motivating and temporary. It is interesting perhaps that this is regarded as a very closed climate for planning and curriculum change (Halpin, 1966). A consultative model may reach many participants and hence foster involvement in planning the curriculum; alternatively, it could be perceived as 'the iron fist in the kid glove', as the locus of power is left undisturbed.

A 'share' decision will be democratic, with authority deriving from expertise (professional rather than positional authority (Bush, 1986)), but it may founder for want of time, or will to participate, or conflict of values. Planners will need to adopt styles which depend on the level of the curriculum debate − conceptual to practical, the type of organizational practices, and the stage of the planning and uptake − from first principles and opening debate to trialling, adoption, implementation and institutionalization.

Levels of Curriculum Management

While this is taken up more in Chapter 2 where levels of planning are established from the contextual to the practical, attention here is drawn to the notion of spheres of influence, levels of decision-making and use of staff expertise. The question requires curriculum planners to harness levels of the curriculum debate and decision-making to staff expertise and power. The task harks back to the style of curriculum management − hierarchical to collegial.

If a hierarchical model is adopted then decision-making power is clear (see Figure 1.1.). If a collegial style is present then equalization of power is its predicate (c.f. Bush, 1986), see Figure 1.2. This latter, or a variation of it which sets the head and deputy above the other scales which remain clustered together, may more fairly reflect the nature of primary schools where teachers regard each other as a community of equals (Lortie, 1975), regardless of the scale posts which may be awarded for curriculum or pastoral responsibilities. For the purposes here, curriculum planners will need to decide which levels and states of the planning debate are best dealt with by which people, external or internal to the school (Lavelle, 1984), and which people will take decisions about which aspects of the

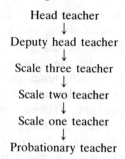

FIGURE 1.1   A hierarchical model of decision-making

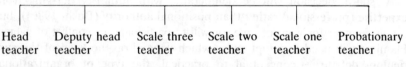

FIGURE 1.2   A collegial model of decision-making

curriculum and its planning. For successful curriculum planning these levels need to mesh, to integrate, in the true spirit of primary education.

EVALUATIVE CONTEXTS

If curriculum planning is to be effective, and if the notion of effectiveness implies both matching, as discussed in later chapters, and curriculum development and renewal, then there is a built-in need to evaluate the curriculum – its planning, implementation and outcomes. Evaluation is the springboard to action, to planning. This need is being increasingly accorded recognition, priority and formalization, both politically and educationally (DES, 1977; 1981; 1983). At a national level this is reflected in the establishment of the Assessment of Performance Unit (APU), the growth of central directives and reports (DES, 1985b; 1985c). At a local level Simons (1984) sees it reflected in increased testing of pupil performance, increasing public reporting by schools (by brochures, headteachers' reports, four yearly reports), curriculum review and institutional evaluation. At an institutional level the emergence of school and teacher evaluation, appraisal and self-evaluation surfaced in the 1970s as a legitimate means of meeting the demand from, and response to, macro pressures for increased teacher accountability. Such pressures rode on the crests of several waves – political, economic and educational.

Initially the economic retrenchment of the 1970s required asssurances from education of 'value for money' (Callaghan, 1976). In the optimism of post-war economic expansion and stability, education was the shining star in the human capital theorists' heaven — that investment in self-development yielded personal and economic satisfaction. At times of economic and fiscal difficulty, given impetus by the 1973 oil crisis, education became the scapegoat for an ailing society, criticized for its tenuous links with industry, its inability to prepare children for the world of work, and its alleged contribution to the relaxing moral fibre of the country's youth. Evaluation then became a form of reassurance (Holt, 1981).

Secondly, in education there was a burgeoning expansion of, and interest in, methods and methodologies of curriculum evaluation *per se*. Well-tried methods operated at the level of national large-scale projects (e.g. Schools Council); new methods emerged (e.g. Parlett and Hamilton,

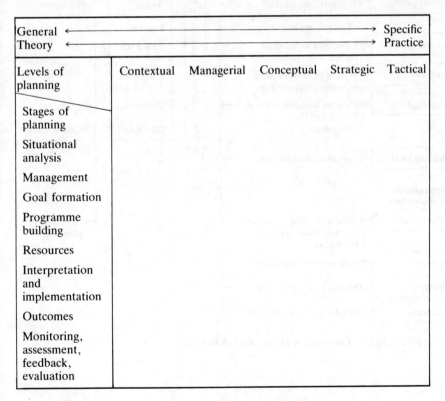

FIGURE 1.3   Levels and stages of curriculum evaluation

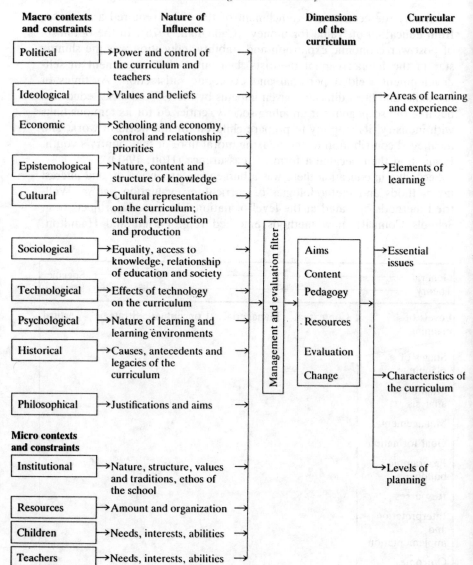

FIGURE 1.4 Components of the curriculum debate

1976), and the alleged merits and demerits of both were severally debated and clarified.

For curriculum planners the urge to evaluate should be strong both because it meets macro-level demands and because at a micro-level effective planning requires constant evaluation and feedback at all stages and levels. Evaluation is both a judgement of worth, of value, and of effectiveness of a proposal or outcome. It is a decision-making process based on analysis and judgements of information collected during the planning period. Evaluation informs and shapes each stage and level of planning (Skilbeck, 1984); this can be extended and portrayed in a two-dimensional model (see Figure 1.3).

What to Evaluate in Curriculum Planning

While the components of Figure 1.3 are analysed in more detail in Chapter 2, curriculum planners will have to debate about purposes, foci, timing and criteria for evaluating each element, the relationship between them, and the use of the evaluations to inform and steer the process of planning. Evaluation then becomes part of a critical debate about a proposal (Kemmis, 1982) rather than an end-of-course assessment, the terms and metaphors (House, 1985) of which debate are set out in subsequent chapters.

In approaching primary curriculum planning, both theoretical and practical issues are brought together at all levels and stages of planning. Planning has to grasp and synthesize into curricular outcomes a variety of concerns and constraints; the problem is one of containing and bounding this variety and translating it into practice. The field of discussion is represented in Figure 1.4. The underlying principles governing the synthesis should be those outlined earlier which make up the primary ethos. How such diffuse concerns are brought together, both conceptually and practically, is the subject of the next chapter.

2
CURRICULUM PLANNING MODELS

Curriculum planning is the translation of value judgements into practice. Chapter 1 provided some conceptual frameworks which underpin planning and which reinforce the view that curriculum planning is not finite; it involves continual questioning of the aims and content of children's learning. One mechanism for translating such principles into practice is through the use of curriculum models.

PROBLEMS OF CURRICULUM MODELS

Models must be useful, they must facilitate clear thinking and planning. Curriculum planning is an all-embracing term, for it comprehends many stages, many levels of abstraction, many levels of application, many foci of analysis; it originates from many different parties and loci of power, and has to meet demands from many sources. It would be invidious to suppose that a curriculum model could address realistically or honestly this range of problems and issues unitarily. Hence the notion of planning curricula with the assistance of models is pluralistic – many models to serve many concerns. The problems raised, then, concern articulation of the dimensions of models and their clarity and appropriacy to the particular task in the curriculum planning process. The dimensions of curriculum planning models must link to the diverse nature of the term 'curriculum' and to the diverse nature of the planning process. What, then, are these dimensions?

A curriculum planning model must be certain of its range: is it referring to the whole curriculum or to a part of it? This begs the enormous question of defining the curriculum and its constituent parts. Definitions are both varied and broad. Some go for comprehensiveness, e.g. Kerr's suggestion of 'all the learning which is planned and guided by the school whether it is carried on in groups or individually, inside or outside the school' (Kerr, 1968, p. 16), and Orlosky's and Smiths's (1978) view of it as the substance of a school's programme.

While such definitions have the attraction of allowing virtually anything into the curriculum, they offer only loose guidelines to thinking about the curriculum: that it must be planned, that it must include the hidden as well as the formal curriculum, and that it must involve a wide field of focus. Such definitions fail to address problems of selection and justification, participants and processes of curriculum planning and implementation. Other definitions err on the other side, being narrow and very tightly prescriptive: e.g. 'a programme of activities designed so that pupils will attain by learning certain specifiable ends or objectives' (Hirst, 1968, p. 40) or the *Oxford English Dictionary* definition as 'a course of study'.

Other definitions attempt to bridge the gap of the broad or the narrow. Skilbeck (1984) defines it as referring 'to the learning of students, in so far as they are expressed or anticipated in educational goals and objectives, plans and designs for learning and the implementation of these plans and designs in school environments' (p. 21).

Definitions of the curriculum thus cannot be relied upon to produce useful guidelines for modelling the curriculum. A curriculum planning model then must make explicit its range. It may contain reference to the whole school — a systemic and complex model (Dalin, 1978) which incorporates:

1. Participants and roles, school organizational, administrative and management structures and networks.
2. Contexts of the curriculum — historical, ideological, philosophical, sociological, cultural, political, psychological, and so on.
3. The relationships of the school and its curriculum to wider society.
4. Curriculum aims, content, pedagogies, resources, evaluation, development strategies and directions.
5. Styles and modes of curriculum planning and dissemination — problem-solving, interactive and centre-periphery (Havelock, 1973).

Alternatively, it may refer to the whole school or to a particular part of the whole curriculum, either specifically, e.g. music or music in the infant years, or more generally, e.g. language across the curriculum. Further, it may refer to an individual teacher's curriculum in general or to an individual teacher's particular area of her or his total curriculum. The implications of being clear on the range of the curriculum being addressed are to point to the level of analysis of the curriculum statement, policy or plan. A whole school curriculum policy statement will almost necessarily be less specific than a curriculum area's or an individual teacher's statement and planning process. This refers back to the level or stage at which the curriculum model is pitched.

A curriculum planning model must be clear on its purpose, whether it is to be prescriptive or descriptive − a 'model for' planning (Figure 2.1) or a 'model of' planning (Figure 2.2). The former portrays, perhaps, an ideal view of curriculum planning − comprehensive and evolutionary − whereas the latter describes actual practice − which may be good or terribly poor. Significantly, the descriptive example overlooks the role of theory, evaluation and modification of theory and practice; it represents *ad hoc* and static curriculum planning. Further, such prescriptive and descriptive models must be clear on the level at which they are prescribing or describing, for planning models range from the contextual to the practical and specific.

It is possible to identify five levels of curriculum planning models

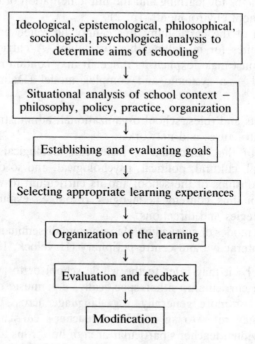

FIGURE 2.1 A prescriptive model of curriculum planning

which move from the general to the specific and from the abstract to the concrete classroom situation (Figure 2.3). It is a brave curriculum planner who attempts to incorporate all levels into a single model, for there are qualitative differences between each.

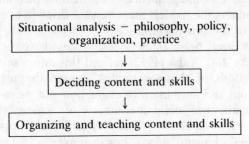

FIGURE 2.2   A descriptive model of curriculum planning

LEVEL ONE: CONTEXTUAL LEVEL

These draw on the contexts set in Chapter 1 and on the primary ethos which it described. They attempt a broad brush approach to factors in the

Theory   General

Level 1: Contextual
          Philosophical, ideological,
          epistemological, sociological,
          cultural, psychological contexts
          of curriculum decisions

Level 2: Managerial
          Substantive issues discussing
          the management of curriculum
          planning

Level 3: Conceptual
          Rationales for describing and
          typifying the curriculum

Level 4: Strategic
          Policy making, staffing and
          resourcing of the curriculum,
          role relations

Level 5: Tactical
          Planning curriculum implementation

Practice   Specific

FIGURE 2.3   Levels of curriculum planning models

planning process. Contextual models have a considerable pedigree in curriculum theory (despite Barrow's (1984) reservations about them); one can discern a clear line from Tyler (1949), through Taba (1962), Wheeler (1967) and Skilbeck (1976a). The essence of models cast in this mould is to establish clear foci and sequence of curriculum planning. For primary curriculum planners the models must be shot through at every stage with the principles of the primary ethos.

Tyler (1949) poses four famous questions as the basis for curriculum planning (Figure 2.4). Taba (1962) refined this into a seven-stage model (Figure 2.5). Both of these examples assume the reasonableness of starting with aims and finishing with evaluation − a means−end model − deciding on ends then designing means to achieve them. This has weaknesses, many of which are well aired (MacDonald-Ross, 1975; Sockett, 1976; Kelly, 1982; Lawton, 1983). For example:

1. Evaluation is seen as terminal (summative) rather than continuous (formative).
2. This model assumes that it is acceptable to determine children's end behaviours at the planning stage of the curriculum − which has the potential to deny their creativity, choice, needs and interests.
3. The educative process is seen as producing solely demonstrable, behavioural outcomes.

1. What educational purposes should the school seek to attain?	**Aims**
2. What educational experiences can be provided that are likely to attain these purposes?	↓
	Content
3. How can these experiences be organized effectively?	↓
4. How can we determine whether these purposes are being met?	**Pedagogy**
	↓
	Evaluation

FIGURE 2.4   Tyler's questions for curriculum planning

1. Diagnosis of needs	**Aims and**
2. Formulation of objectives	**Objectives**
3. Selection of content	↓
4. Organization of content	**Content**
5. Selection of learning experiences	↓
6. Organization of learning experiences	**Pedagogy**
7. Determination of what to evaluate and means of doing it	↓
	Evaluation

FIGURE 2.5   Taba's seven-stage model of curriculum planning

4. This clearly prescriptive model neglects the actual way in which teachers plan their work; they do not commence with aims and then plan in the order stated.

Skilbeck (1982) attempts to reduce the excesses of this model by three means. His model is represented in Figure 2.6. The model includes two obvious improvements in Tyler and Taba; his inclusion of a fully fledged 'situational analysis' as an element of curriculum planning is an addition to the Tyler model; a situational analysis requiring an examination and incorporation of the contexts of curriculum planning outlined in Chapter 1 and of internal pressures and constraints on curriculum planners. This ties curriculum planning firmly to the 'reconceptualist' notion (Pinar, 1975) that a curriculum is unique to a specific school and a group of teachers and pupils at a specific time and place.

Second, Skilbeck's feedback loop to reviewing the situation and situational analysis adds a dimension absent in Tyler — the need to reconsider and reformulate aims and objectives. His third modification is not immediately apparent. Skilbeck encourages users to enter the model at the stage which is appropriate to their perceived needs; it is not necessary here to begin with aims and objectives. Similarly, he argues that users may go through the components in any order, even running some elements in tandem. The significance of this third point is striking; Skilbeck is breaking the mould of Tyler and replacing a prescriptive stage theory

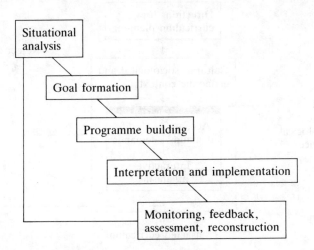

FIGURE 2.6   Skilbeck's curriculum development model

model with a more overtly interactive model. Interaction is assumed in the Tyler model, but it is in one direction only.

In Skilbeck's model participants are freer, more creative and responsive agents of planning; key elements of his model are mutually interacting. Skilbeck, though perhaps silent in his model on persons and their agency, sets the scene for explicit interactive models of curriculum planning; this can be taken forward into a proposal for an interactive model of curriculum planning at a high level of abstraction (Figure 2.7). This model sets interaction at the heart of the planning process. It embodies the heart of the curriculum reconceptualists' belief in the primacy of situated activity and the value of individuals' autobiographies entering the curriculum planning process. The teacher, embedded in cultures and social contexts, and through her or his perceptions of organizational constraints and own psychological make-up, addresses the pressures to follow directions in curriculum planning, accepting, modifying and resisting such demands.

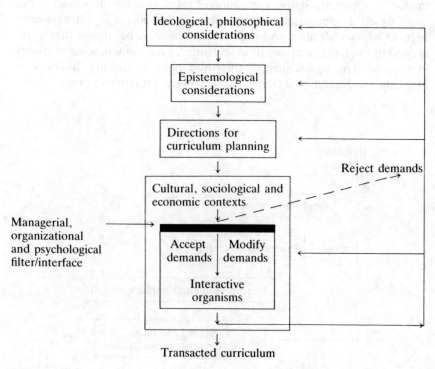

FIGURE 2.7   An interactive model of curriculum planning

The teacher can offer feedback to review ideology, epistemology and philosophy. Such a model accords importance to a neglected area of curriculum planning — the personal and interpersonal dynamic and dialectic — long established in change and innovation theory (see Chapter 1; Havelock, 1973; Hoyle, 1975a), but relatively poorly articulated in theories of planning (Pinar and Grumet, 1981).

Just as in change theory the interpersonal dimension has received growing attention, so in successful planning there must be a focus on the planners, participants and recipients. Thus the concept of the curriculum in Chapter 1 as being open, negotiable and problematic is kept wide, negotiation being (1) among the participants, (2) within each participant and planner, and (3) between planners, participants and recipients. The need for this negotiation is felt as sharply among teachers in internally generated curriculum planning as if it were to be externally generated.

LEVEL TWO: MANAGERIAL LEVEL

This has been discussed in Chapter 1, and the factors in the management of curriculum planning can be represented in Figures 2.8 and 2.9.

LEVEL THREE: CONCEPTUAL LEVEL

Curriculum planning needs to decide its definition of the curriculum. The Schools Council (1983) alludes to this when attempting to describe the curriculum in five ways:

1. The curriculum as subjects, e.g. English, mathematics, science, history. The strength of such a conception lies in its ability to enable teachers quickly to ascertain whether children are following a broad or a narrow curriculum. Similarly, children identify them easily. Whether describing

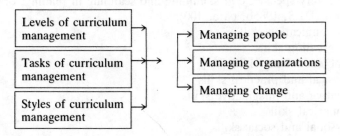

FIGURE 2.8 Dimensions of management of curriculum planning

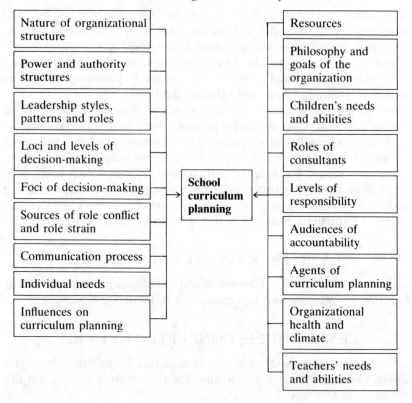

FIGURE 2.9   Management factors in curriculum planning

the curriculum by subjects represents more a secondary than a primary style is open to debate.

2. The curriculum as process, i.e. a focus on skills teaching. Such skills can be very specific, e.g. skimming and scanning in reading, or more general (DES, 1985b, para. 100):

    communication skills
    observation skills
    problem-solving skills
    physical and practical skills
    creative and imaginative skills
    numerical skills
    personal and social skills

The notion of a skill involves practice as well as direct instruction. These skills link closely to the primary ethos detailed in Chapter 1.

3. The curriculum as the study of problems. These are issues facing pupils for the late twentieth and twenty-first centuries, e.g. multi-ethnic societies, computer literacy, Third World studies, ecology, conservation, pollution and energy utilization. The proportion of the timetable which could, or should, be devoted to this is debatable as ideological pressures differ; conservative ideologies would underplay this area while reconstructionist- and society-focused ideologies would stress it.

4. The curriculum as areas of knowledge and experience. The problems of the origins of these areas have already been hinted at in Chapter 1 — whether their roots lie in epistemology, culture, tradition, or accepted practice. Given such discrepant sources it is scarcely surprising to find different classifications of what worthwhile knowledge should be taught (see Table 2.1). While there are clear discrepancies between the representations, it is striking how similar they all are. Indeed, they collectively and severally can be used as frameworks for common curricula (c.f. Proctor, 1984). The notion of areas of experience rather than bodies of knowledge accords perhaps more clearly that other conceptions with the value of experiences stressed in the primary ethos.

5. The curriculum through a child's eyes — a much neglected area, but one which emphasizes sensory experiences, friendships, locations, activities and enjoyments, i.e. the hidden curriculum. Such a perspective throws into sharp relief the problems of match — matching the teacher's intentions and curriculum planning with the perceptions and understandings which the child brings to, and takes from, the curriculum experience.

An alternative way of describing the curriculum has been suggested by Scrimshaw (1983), who offers five categories of the substance of children's learning:

1. Facts, beliefs, statements and theories, i.e. cognitive or academic learning.
2. Policies, principles and rules, i.e. learning social behaviour.
3. Ideas and concepts, i.e. an emphasis on understanding.
4. Skills, activities and actions, i.e. those areas which emphasize doing rather than reflecting.
5. Insights, feelings, emotions, attitudes and habits, i.e. development of the personality. This has resonances with the DES (1985b) which reinforce the need to consider 'elements of learning' in curriculum planning — knowledge, concepts, skills and attitudes.

An alternative to the previous conceptions can be found in a classroom-learning-based model (Ridley and Trembath, 1986). This draws on content,

TABLE 2.1 A chronology of representations of the curriculum as areas of knowledge or experience

Peterson (1975)	Phenix (1975)	Hirst (1965)	Lawton (1973)
Logical	Symbolics (languages, maths, logic)	Mathematics	Mathematics
Empirical	Empirics (physical and social sciences)	Physical sciences	Sciences
Moral	Aesthetics (arts)	Human sciences	Aesthetics and creative
Aesthetic	Synnoetics (relational insight)	History	Physical
	Ethics (morals)	Religion	Social and political
	Synoptics (history, religion and philosophy)	Literature and fine arts	Ethical
		Philosophy	Linguistic
			Spiritual

DES (1977)	DES (1978a)	CDC (1980)	Galton, Simon and Croll (1980)
Mathematical	Mathematics	Arts and crafts	Mathematics
Linguistic	Language and literacy	Communication	Language
Scientific	Science	Health education	Arts and craft
Social and political	Aesthetic and physical	Environmental studies	General studies (RE, history, geography, social studies, science)
Physical	Social studies	Work, leisure and lifestyle	
Ethical		Mathematical skills and reasoning and their applications	
Aesthetic and creative		Scientific and technological ways of knowing and their application	
		Social, cultural and civic studies	
		Moral reasoning and action, value and belief systems	

DES (1982b)
Mathematics
Language and literacy
Religious and moral
  education
Learning about people
Learning about the physical
  world
Learning about materials,
  plants and animals
Art and craft
Music
PE

Lawton (1983)
Social system
Economic system
Communication system
Rationality system
Technology system
Moral system
Belief system
Aesthetic system

DES (1983)
Mathematics
Language and literacy
Science
Modern languages
Music
Arts and crafts
Home studies
Physical health education
History
Geography and RE

DES (1985b)
Aesthetic and creative
Human and social
Linguistic and literary
Mathematical
Moral
Physical
Scientific
Spiritual
Technological

skills, concepts, problem-solving, interests and objects, pointing the way to level five models (tactical levels). It is rooted in practical applicability, thus providing a bridge from theoretical concerns and practical outcomes; the abstract to the concrete (Figure 2.10).

The model accommodates activity-centred approaches and at the same time recognizes the importance of knowledge within the process of learning. It points clearly to the importance of direct experiences coupled with the centrality of skills, the involvement and development of the child's personality and yet a concern for outcomes and products. It is a model which takes account of two significant polarities in describing the curriculum outlined earlier in the chapter – the curriculum as planned by the teacher and the curriculum through the child's eyes. It is thus a model which lies at the interface of theory and children's classroom experiences. It has a clear sympathy with the primary ethos outlined earlier, where conservative

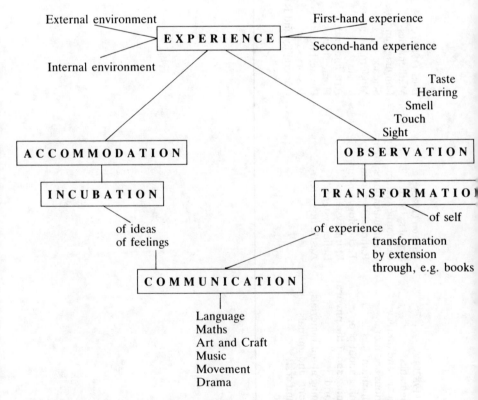

FIGURE 2.10   A classroom-learning model of curriculum planning

and instrumental ideologies are tempered with child-centredness and progressivism.

Conceptual levels of modelling the curriculum, then, are devolved upon decision-making about the structuring and classification of knowledge for children.

LEVEL FOUR: STRATEGIC LEVEL

This level synthesizes the previous three levels, analyzing personnel deployment, roles, resources and their optimal use, translating values and general organization of knowledge in the curriculum into specific policies at a whole staff level, i.e. tailored to a school's individual situation. It is represented in Figure 2.11 (c.f. Hicks, 1972). At this fourth level collective and individual responsibility for curriculum planning looks to all three previous levels for articulation of key rationales of, and problems and possibilities in, planning the curriculum, and to level five of individual teachers' curriculum planning and implementation. It must be responsive to constraints from all levels. Hence the model translates into school curriculum decision-making policy the interactive model outlined earlier at a contextual level.

LEVEL FIVE: TACTICAL LEVEL

The fifth level of the curriculum modelling process engages class teachers' planning in the long term, medium term, day-to-day and lesson-by-lesson stages. It is informed by all four previous levels, and reciprocally informs them. There are six typifications of curriculum planning at this level. They cover planning which is content-based, skills-based, problem-based, interest-based, objectives-based (c.f. Barnes 1982), activity-based, theme-based, informed by a 'classroom learning model'. A full curriculum plan will need to draw eclectically on all types.

Content-based Planning

Here the teacher approaches curriculum planning by examining the possibilities for learning in an identifiable corpus of content in terms of:

1. Activities.
2. Concepts.
3. Information to be emphasized.
4. Resources.

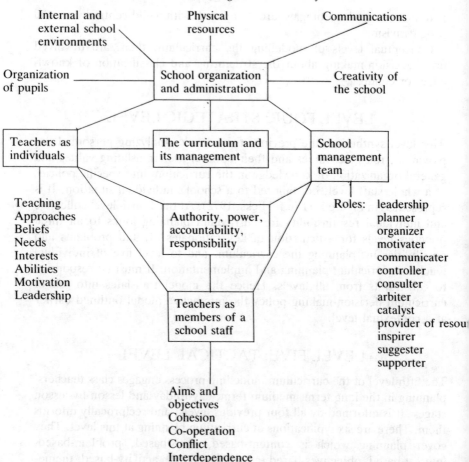

FIGURE 2.11 Dimensions of curriculum policy-making at school level

The origin of the content is problematic here. Does it derive from epistemology, a cultural analysis, or a child-centred ideology of what is engaging the child at a particular moment of time?

The question of who makes the selection is problematic; be it teachers, children, HMI, advisers, DES, governors or parents, there will be power and potential conflict brought into the curriculum arena.

Similarly, the form or expression of that content is problematic. Is it best expressed in areas of experience, subjects, schemas, concepts or processes? Taba (1962) offers some guidelines here, suggesting that at its lowest level content can be expressed in terms of specific facts and processes. At the next level it can be expressed in terms of basic principles – the structure of a subject (however defined; see Chapter 1); at its third level it comprises concepts – abstract ideas built up through a variety of experiences. At its highest level it constitutes thought systems and methods of enquiry; Taba here betrays a sympathy to the discipline-centred approach to curriculum planning outlined by Hirst (1965). If one adopts a content based approach to curriculum planning, Barnes (1982) suggests that it can be staged thus:

1. Select the content.
2. Express the concepts and principles which arise out of the content.
3. Prioritize content and concepts.
4. Sequence the learning.
5. Contruct a web diagram of the content.
6. Scrutinize the content to see how far it allows children to perceive links between areas – concept formation. This refers to the 'curriculum through the child's eyes' discussed earlier.
7. List resources.

A web diagram is problematic, many webs comprise either low-level facts and ideas or fail to make clear the levels of generality outlined earlier by Taba; they mix low-order and high-order facts and principles unselfconsciously; e.g. Figure 2.12. In this example it is evident that content is expressed in terms of activities, information, concepts, methods and methodologies (e.g. the 'scientific method'). This model is undeveloped; it is exploratory and expositional rather than thorough, ordered and structured. It is not easy to discern how low and higher order thinking can be developed and structured through the work; it is by no means exhaustive in the key areas identified in terms of their potential to develop activities, information, basic principles, concepts and methods of enquiry.

An improved version is portrayed in Figure 2.13. Not only is this more detailed but the detail reveals a clear conception and application of Taba's four levels of content expression. The application is comprehensive, i.e. it applies to all three areas described, the model is sequenced, and the cross-references give it coherence. A web diagram, then, will need to address areas of the curriculum, levels of thinking, activities, concepts, skills, knowledge, teaching and learning styles. Planning the curriculum by content makes for a potentially relevant curriculum; it compels teachers to analyse key concepts of curriculum programmes, can allow for progression and continuity, breadth and balance (DES, 1985b) and assists in the avoidance of repetition (Blyth *et al*, 1976).

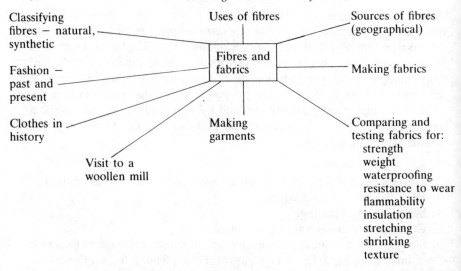

FIGURE 2.12   A web diagram on 'fibres and fabrics'

There are, however, difficulties with this model. Constructing a curriculum from a statement of content may be completely arbitrary, incoherent with the rest of the curriculum, biased, conservative, a received rather than a reflexive curriculum (Eggleston, 1977), neglectful of aims and objectives (purposeless), potentially neglectful of processes and skills, potentially closed to new knowledge, and certainly neglectful of the whole issue of matching.

Concept-based Planning

Here the starting point is a concept rather than a body of knowledge, e.g. rhythm, power, change, balance. The concept can straddle few or many subject fields. The concept-based approach shares many of the advantages and disadvantages of the content-based approach. Additionally, the strength of this approach is its fittingness to the elements of the primary ethos which stress integration of knowledge and meeting the whole personality of the child. The major drawback of this approach concerns 'the curriculum through the child's eyes': to what extent will the integration be in the teacher's rather than the child's mind; to what extent is it acceptable or possible to attempt to integrate completely different, and often exclusive, disciplines in a way which is not contrived or artificial? For example, the concept of 'power' mentioned earlier will have completely different

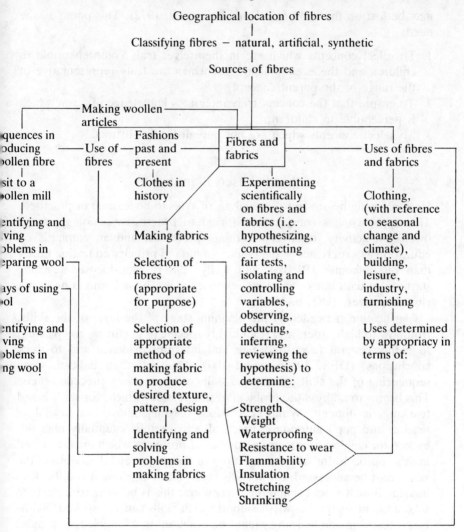

FIGURE 2.13 A completed web diagram on 'fibres and fabrics'

meanings for the social scientist, the historian, the musician, the religious educator, the scientist, the mathematician, the artist or the physical education teacher. How can these different perspectives realistically hope to be integrated or perceived in any unitary way by the child? The term 'power' is no more than a convenient label whose integrated meaning may be lost on the child (c.f. Schools Council, 1972). This points to the need:

1. To select concepts which are in themselves truly comprehensible to children and the exemplification of which are truly representative of the range of the parent concept.
2. To ensure that the concept truly integrates knowledge in a way which is perceptible to children.
3. To select concepts which are not unrealistically abstract.

Skills-based Planning

Here planning begins from an analysis of skills to be learned or practised. This approach has considerable appeal to progressive ideology, for it dwells on activity, discovery learning, processes, and an emphasis on education as experience – the empiricist base of primary education rather than on outcomes (Blenkin and Kelly, 1981): 'Skill-focused teaching starts from data not conclusions, experience not books, and is open not closed' (Oliver, 1982, p. 131).

Clarification is needed at the planning stage of the level of the skills; from low to high order, and from highly specific (e.g. cutting and pasting) to highly general (e.g. 'to weigh and interpret evidence and to draw conclusions' (DES, 1985b, para. 100). This will then indicate some sequencing of the skills; that some skills will necessarily precede others. This begins to address the problem of progression, which, for skills-based teaching, is difficult. While skills-based teaching allows for flexibility, teacher and pupil autonomy, practical activity and potentially high relevance for children, there are a number of problems which must be faced in this approach. Initially the questions of the origins and directions of the skills must be addressed, for in skills-based teaching alone it is difficult to imagine how it would shape the curriculum; this is because it neglects to take account of the knowledge upon which skills can be worked. Skills-based teaching and learning cannot be practised in a knowledge vacuum; a pure skills-based approach simply does not address the questions of content, of deciding worthwhile knowledge, or of planning for the development and progression of knowledge. Its neglect of the knowledge dimension and its failure to address knowledge outcomes of skills could render the curriculum static and offer little guidance or basis for future curriculum development. The relationship between skills and knowledge must be drawn. Further, in considering the origins of the skills-based curriculum, there is the question of decision-making; who decides on the skills to be learned, taught or practised? If it is left to individuals alone then it runs the risk of being arbitrary − at the whim of decision-makers − which may fortuitously produce a broad and interesting curriculum, but which may also produce a curriculum which is narrow and lustreless.

There is a further problem in that evaluation of the skill development might either be trivial (focusing solely on the observable and the measurable) or over complex (focusing on the abstract, general and unobservable) which constitutes much of education. The direction in which skills-based planning points is to show initially its useful contribution to curriculum planning but its overall inadequacy as a total model for structuring and developing the curriculum.

There is perhaps a more acceptable alternative in the concept of a process approach to planning (Stenhouse, 1975). Planning the curriculum on a process model attempts to insert rigour into the pure skills-based model, to render less arbitrary the skills developed, and to move away from the simplistic view that skills alone can determine curriculum planning. It seeks to show that instead of skills being the starting point, curriculum planning can begin, so to speak, from the other end; that by studying the content and the structure of that content, certain skills will suggest themselves as being appropriate to the learning of that content, and consistent with the significant features of that content. This model addresses both the problem of knowledge and its selection, and principles of pedagogy. It marries progressive ideologies and those ideologies which emphasize a concern for knowledge.

For example, in music teaching the content of music concerns, among other factors, performances, appreciation and composition. It is suggested in the process approach that the skills required of children for a full understanding of these factors would be those of actual performance, appreciation and composition. The skills derive from an analysis of content and not vice versa. Similarly, in science teaching scientific methodology is premissed on the notion that scientific ideas and concepts are in principle falsifiable, that scientific knowledge is provisional; the scientist formulates a hypothesis, tests it and reviews the hypothesis, fitting it into a paradigmatic framework or reformulating the paradigm. Hence in science teaching, to be true to this methodology and rationale, children must be immersed in the scientific, critical method rather than simply accepting scientific 'facts' unquestioningly.

A further, much celebrated, example of the 'process' approach is the Humanities Curriculum Project (Stenhouse, 1968), which focused on controversial issues in society − war, poverty, race − open-ended matters for which there are no clear or finite answers. Given that the content is open-ended and in a sense indecisive or inconclusive, then the skills and pedagogy deriving from that content must be appropriate to dealing with that type of content. Hence the project decided that discussion was a principal teaching method, a principal skill to be learned and practised, and that, as neither teachers nor pupils could claim to possess the 'right' answers to controversial issues, the teacher should be a neutral chairperson, and that children should be learning skills of posing questions and prompting debate, articulating and reflecting rather than seeking fixed solutions to open problems. If the content were investigative and exploratory then the skills appropriate to that content should be investigative and exploratory.

One has to question here whether the process model suffers from the spectres of Tyler's and Taba's linear models of curriculum planning — with implicit objectives (Hirst, 1980; Skilbeck, 1984) and the selection of learning experiences appropriate to the content. Other problems ensue in the process model, notably that of assessment, for the teacher is cast into the role of diagnoser and critical friend rather than marker; a process rather than a product concern. Futher, the question has to be raised of its suitability for all areas of the curriculum; is it perhaps only suited to the humanities and social science areas? Like the content-based model, it too does not question the origin of the content; it may be completely arbitrary. Thus, though there are considerable attractions to the process approach, as a model for curriculum planning it is incomplete.

Problem-based Planning

Here emphasis is placed on children solving problems responsibly, e.g. a multiplicity of problems can be identified in mathematics, CDT, environmental studies or drama. In this approach teachers must be clear on seven points. Initially the educational aims of the problem-solving activity must be approached to clarify whether the emphasis is to be on the solution or on the process. This requires teachers to clarify whether they are in fact engaged in problem-solving or investigational work where a solution is not necessary. It also begs the question of whether in fact the problem is soluble; teachers in their planning must determine this as it will affect the aims of the activity, its criteria for success and resources to be used.

Second, teachers must be clear on the extent to which problem-solving approaches can become the basis for whole curriculum planning; are there some areas of the curriculum which do not readily lend themselves to problem-solving approaches? It is fundamental here to determine whether the problem-solving approach to planning concerns the aims of the curriculum or the pedagogical processes; whether the intention here is to develop in children the facility either to regard learning and behaviour from a solely problem-solving basis or to recognize that problem-solving is a useful method of tackling certain situations − a strategy rather than an aim. One has to question here whether, realistically, all learning could be problem-solving, as:

1. Children depend on past experience to recognize problems (Entwistle, 1970).
2. Time pressures in school may prevent this ideal from becoming reality.

Third, the expression of the problem must be clarified. The problem must be clearly recognized, identified and operationalized, i.e. expressed in a way which suggests pathways to its solution. This will involve identifying key factors which cause the problem. For example, children might be investigating the problem of lack of leisure time amenities in their locality. It would be unacceptable to tackle this solely at the level of complaint ('there's not enough to do in the evenings'); it would need explication and exegesis, for example:

1. Is the problem lack of amenities or is it something else?
2. What are the alternatives to providing amenities?
3. Who is registering the complaints and why?
4. What are the aims of providing the amenities?
5. What are the present amenities?
6. How are they used?
7. Why are they not used or abused?
8. Who uses the present amenities?
9. What objections would there be to increasing amenities?
10. What additional amenities are required?
11. Whom would the additional amenities serve?
12. What are the advantages and disadvantages of proposed sitings?
13. How would they be financed?
14. On what criteria would provision be prioritized?

Fourth, the level of complexity of the problem must be anticipated, as it will affect the sequencing of the problem. For example, the problem of building a model house is far less complex than the planning, construction and arrangement of a model village. Fifth, related to the complexity of the problem is the range of the problem, for example, macro problems (perhaps those relating to Third World poverty, or housing and education in developing countries, or human rights) dwarf more localized problems. Attempts to address such problems might not be able to go beyond the superficial level in schools. This links to the sixth consideration, the extent to which the problem is realistically within the capabilities of children and teachers to comprehend and solve. Finally, there is the ideological question of who generates the problems. Are they teachers' or children's problems? If they are children's problems are they then perceived as such by the children? Thus the notion of problem-solving planning is itself problematic. While it may in fact describe more accurately than a didactic model the ways in which children learn, like other approaches, it does not straightforwardly provide a model which teachers and planners can accept at face value.

Interest-based Planning

Here work follows a particular interest or event, for example, the child's interests or a visit, a collection, a theatrical experience and so on. This form of planning is opportunistic, is overtly related to child-centredness, and provides for high pupil involvement and relevance. It respects pupil freedoms and choices; it is a model which is perhaps common practice in nursery and infant education, sadly reducing as children progress through the primary years. Its merits are clear. However, there are difficulties and problematic areas in this approach. Interests may be unsuitable or incomplete as basis for curriculum planning (Dearden, 1968; Hirst and Peters, 1970). The curriculum could become completely random, partial and fragmented.

The question is raised, then, of whether, like problem-based planning, the notion of interest-based planning is reflected more in the pedagogy than in the aims. Further, there is an ambivalence in the term 'interests' (Peters, 1966). It comprises both what interests the child and what is in the child's interests. The ambivalence is important for it reveals the decision-making process in the teacher–pupil relationship; a child's interests may be trivial, worthless, ephemeral, horrible, damaging or of limited educational value (see Chapter 1). It is part of the teacher's role to guide the child into developing what is in her or his interests and to see what is of value, be this unacceptable because of its instrumental ideological overtones or not.

For the curriculum planner who likes the security of predetermined outcomes, planning the curriculum by interests is not a suitable model, for the notion of novelty and uncertainty is inherent in it (c.f. Wilson, 1971). Its opportunistic appeal can be viewed as a strength or a drawback, dependent on one's ideological position. How one builds breadth, balance, coverage, consistency, structure, continuity and progression into interest-based planning is also difficult, as are timetabling and resource implications.

The problem then – as with all the previous models outlined by Barnes (1982) – is their exclusivity and partiality. The curriculum planner, seeking comprehensive guidance has thus to focus not only on what models address but what they neglect, and to realize that within each model no glib prescriptions or straightforward guidance can be found. This again reinforces the notion of the need for teachers to be eclectic, reflective and discerning.

Objectives-based Planning

Here teachers begin from a clear specification of what they hope to achieve, or what the pupils will have learned or be able to do by the end of the lesson(s). Objectives describe the hoped-for outcomes of education and curricula (Wiles and Bondi, 1984). The field of objectives-based planning and its relationship to aims, ideology and epistemology is vast. Planners need to consider the following:

1. The desirability and dangers of objectives-based planning.
2. The practicability of objectives-based planning.
3. The applicability of objectives-based planning to all areas of the curriculum.
4. The need to tailor objectives to the ages, abilities, needs and interests of children.
5. The scope of objectives – their range (high to low order, from specific to general, and from specifying products to specifying skills and processes (Figure 2.14)).

While objectives make for clarity of thinking, there is a risk of confining education to that which can be stated specifically, of neglecting both the unobservable and the more spontaneous activities which make classrooms exciting, and of rendering the child a passive recipient of prepared experiences rather than an active creator of those experiences. There are powerful arguments both for and against objectives, and a clear need to clarify their nature, purpose, scope and potential. Such considerations are dealt with in Chapter 3.

This chapter has demonstrated that attempts to translate rationales of the curriculum into practice can be approached through the application of curriculum planning models. Modelling the curriculum is not straightforward. Models clarify and conceptualize but do not themselves provide simple solutions; each model is problematic. This is desirable, for it underlines one of the central themes of this book, that good teaching is not premissed on the uncritical application of a series of practices, but that constantly it is a reflexive and enquiring activity. The problematic

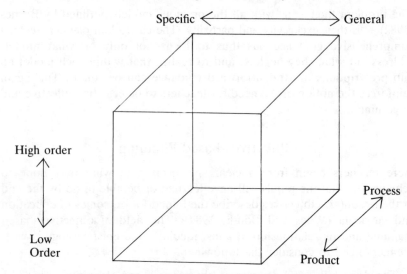

FIGURE 2.14   The scope of objectives in curriculum planning

areas of teaching must be interrogated continually, School learning is
about planned learning, planned learning that is at the same time organized and sequenced but also flexible and responsive to immediate and
unpredictable situations. It is interactional, dependent on the interrelationships between the teacher, the child, the context and the task.
Hence no single blueprint for planning can be proposed, rather a series of
issues can be outlined which planners need to address and use selectively
in the way unique to their situation and purposes. Planners need to
establish frameworks of concerns within which space is created for flexibility, teacher autonomy and development.

3

AIMS AND OBJECTIVES

Primary curriculum planning must know where it is going and why; education is not an aimless activity, it is purposive and intentional (Hirst and Peters, 1970). As such there are aims implicit in the curriculum. The intention of this chapter is to present a conceptual analysis of aims and objectives, to clarify the relationship between aims and objectives, and to discuss their place in the planning of the curriculum.

NATURE AND PURPOSE OF EDUCATIONAL AIMS

There is no single aim of education; education is multidimensional and defined in a variety of ways, and it would be unreasonable to expect one aim to embody or reflect this. A popular analogy is to regard aims as targets (Schofield, 1972), identifiable and reachable. If this analogy is examined then the implication is that once one has fired the curriculum missile at the target then the flight of that missile is beyond the control of the firer. As a model for education this is weak on four counts. First, teachers rightly would resent the notion of the means or processes to the achievement of the aims, the target, being out of their control, the very nature of teaching implies the controlled transmission or discovery of knowledge.

Second, children and teachers interact with each other (Pollard, 1985), constantly shaping their own and each other's futures and situations. To suggest that teachers could plan a curriculum and not have to modify and refashion it in the light of changing situations and interactions is irresponsible and unrealistic, and neglects a key premiss that children develop in ways not always anticipated at the start of an educational programme. The primary ethos is against such behaviouristic prescriptivism.

Third, the notion of aims as targets is poor in that it suggests that aims are in fact reachable; in epistemological terms this means the learning of an identifiable and prespecified body of knowledge whose ideology would perhaps be conservative. The roots and bases for the primary curriculum are not as exclusive as this; they incorporate empiricism as well as rationalism, progressivism as well as instrumentalism or conservatism, processes as well as products. The notion of finite aims lies ill at ease with progressive ideology or empiricist epistemology, for they are by definition open-ended and available for negotiation. In this sense aims are perhaps better regarded as signposts rather than targets; to be educated is not to have arrived, it is to travel with a different view (Peters, 1973) – the transformation criterion of education (Barrow and Woods, 1982). Aims express intentions and purposes rather than explicitly achievable ends. They are long term and generalized (Higginbottom, 1976).

This highlights a fourth significant feature in discussing aims as targets: the relationship between aims and the concept of education. It has been argued (Ryle, 1949) that the concept of education has to be regarded in both 'task' and 'achievement' senses. This has resonances with Passmore (1980) who discusses teaching as an 'attempt-word' and a 'success-word'; for example, teaching someone swimming is a 'task' or 'attempt' whereas actually teaching her or him to swim implies success or achievement, as in 'I taught him to swim' or 'I taught her to drive'.

If 'education' is taken in this 'achievement' sense then problems are raised, for though teachers' aims might be to educate children they might be unsuccessful (Peters, 1973). Indeed, it is suggested that difficulty and distance – their long-term nature – are endemic to notions of aims (Hirst and Peters, 1970), echoing the Plowden report's comments that statements of aims tend to be little more than expressions of benevolent aspirations. Alternatively, education can be regarded as a 'task' word, stressing the doing rather than necessarily the successful outcome – seeking as opposed to finding, educating as opposed to education – clearly a process view which has sympathy with the primary ethos.

There is a clear lesson here that education should be used in both 'attempt' and 'success' terms, 'task' and 'achievement' senses. A problem is raised in using 'education' as a 'task' word, in that this could betray a solely instrumental view of education (Langford, 1968), where education serves some extrinsic purpose or aim, for instance to produce a socialized adult or a suitable candidate for the labour market. This contention has been censured (Brubacher, 1962; Peters, 1966, 1973; Barrow and Woods,

1982), particularly with reference to the primary ethos, where education is regarded as intrinsically worthwhile, having no end beyond itself, being its own end. Hence from this perspective it is more fitting perhaps to discuss aims *in* education rather than aims *of* education.

If education is to comprehend both 'task' and 'achievement' senses, if it is to be predicated on intrinsic and extrinsic value, then there are four clear implications of this for curriculum planners. Initially, the notion of an aim as finite and achievable will have to be replaced by a version which regards aims as statements of desirable processes or criteria − coterminous with values (Ormell, 1980). Indeed, it is this sense that comes out clearly in statements of aims:

1. To acquire knowledge, skills and practical abilities, and the will to use them.
2. To develop qualities of mind, body, spirit, feeling and imagination.
3. To appreciate human achievements in art, music, science, technology and literature.
4. To acquire understanding of the social, economic and political order, and a reasoned set of attitudes, values and beliefs.
5. To prepare for their adult lives at home, at work, at leisure and at large, as consumers and citizens.
6. To develop a sense of self-respect, the capacity to live as independent, self-motivated adults and the ability to function as contributory members of co-operative groups.

(Schools Council, 1981, p.16)

Education becomes an open-ended, ongoing, lifelong activity (Peters, 1966), and the curriculum and its aims must reflect that. Second, the curriculum planner will have to clarify the extent to which instrumental concerns are uppermost in designing the activity. Clearly an activity can serve extrinsic and intrinsic aims simultaneously, for instance reading can be useful, fulfilling and enjoyable. In being clear on the instrumental or intrinsic value of the activity, the curriculum planner will be able to ensure breadth of the curriculum − breadth comprising breadth of justification and purpose as well as expression.

Third, the curriculum planner will have to clarify whether the planned activity lays emphasis on 'task' or 'achievement', for upon this rationale will hinge criteria for evaluation of pupils' learning. It would be inappropriate to condemn a child for an unacceptable product if the intention of the activity lay elsewhere. Finally, the effect of casting attention to the 'task' as well as the 'achievement' aspect of an activity is to reinforce the primary ethos outlined at the end of Chapter 1; it is possible to discern a link between intrinsic value, processes, tasks and progressive ideology on the one hand, and a link between extrinsic value, achievements, instrumentalism and conservative ideologies on the other. Aims, then, can be regarded as general statements of long-term intentions, derived from value systems which may lie outside the immediate school context, being inexpressible in finite or achievable terms. Their appropriate and characteristic usage is to preface whole curriculum statements or courses or programmes of activities, for example:

1. To help pupils to develop lively, enquiring minds, the ability to question and argue rationally and to apply themselves to tasks, and physical skills.
2. To help pupils to acquire knowledge and skills relevant to adult life and employment in a fast-changing world.
3. To help pupils to use language and number effectively.
4. To instil respect for religious and moral values, and tolerance of other races, religions, and ways of life.
5. To help pupils to understand the world in which they live, and the interdependence of individuals, groups and nations.
6. To help pupils to appreciate human achievements and aspirations.

(DES, 1981, para. 11)

The Curriculum Development Centre (CDC, 1980) offers its own list of aims of education:

1. The nurturing and development of the powers of reasoning, reflective and critical thinking, imagining, feeling and communicating among and between persons.
2. The maintenance, development and renewal (and not merely the preservation) of the culture; that is of our forms and systems of thought, meaning and expression — such as scientific knowledge, the arts, language and technology.
3. The maintenance, development and renewal (and not merely preservation of) the social, economic and political order — including its underlying values, fundamental structures and institutions.
4. The promotion of mental, physical, spiritual and emotional health in all people.

(Curriculum Development Centre, 1980, p. 9)

CLASSIFYING AIMS

Aims vary according to their focus and to the concept of education held by curriculum planners. For example, if education is conceived of as training then the aims of the curriculum will emphasize the successful performance of a particular set of skills; if education is conceived of as instruction then successful retention of information might be stressed. However, if the concept of education is broader than this, emphasizing either induction into the thought systems of a culture and a society or initiation into social values and norms, then the parameters of the aims will be necessarily wider (Stenhouse, 1975). If this is so then one would expect to see perhaps conflicting discussions and conceptualizations of aims, particularly if the origins of aims are seen to reside in values and ideological systems. This reinforces the view of Hartnett and Naish (1976) that education is an 'essentially contested concept'. Value systems will represent a view of society, a view of culture, a view of knowledge, a view of the individual and a view of education. If one considers the potential for disagreement among value systems and their holders' aims for education, e.g. those of the DES, local education authorities (LEA), industrialists, employers, academics, parents, pupils and teachers, one would hardly be surprised to find conflicting statements and priorities (c.f. Lawton, 1984). Yet statements of educational aims are marked by consistency and consensus (e.g. DES, 1985b). This is scarcely surprising perhaps as, by their general nature, aims will bind together disparate values and interests:

> education has certain long-term goals. They are first, to enlarge a child's knowledge, experience and imaginative understanding, and thus his awareness of moral values and capacity for enjoyment; and second, to enable him to enter the world after formal education is over as an active participant in the society and a responsible contributor to it, capable of achieving as much independence as possible .... The purpose of education for all children is the same; the goals are the same. But the help that individual children need in progressing towards them will be different.
>
> (DES, 1978b, para. 14)

There are dangers in accepting this broad consensual view of aims (Whitty, 1985), for it may be that it suppresses the valuable debate about conflict; it conceals fundamentally conflicting ideologies, allowing perhaps the hegemony of the dominant ideology to suffuse the educational system unquestioned. It may be thus more productive to maintain difference rather than to swamp it in consensual terminology and statement.

How then can curriculum planners organize their thinking about aims? One common means is by discussing aims which refer to individual development and aims which refer to the needs of society (Ashton, Kneen, and Davies, 1975), acknowledging that they are not mutually exclusive (Central Advisory Council for Education (CACE), 1967; White, 1982b). However, the dichotomy is untenable and erroneous; education does not serve either one or the other; the child inextricably belongs to a culture, a society; children do not lose their individuality by serving society, indeed the opposite may be true. This latter point is well recognized by Plowden where the best preparation for a happy and useful life is seen as being founded on a fulfilled childhood.

Alternatively, Ashton, Kneen and Davies (1975) analyse aims through a matrix (Figure 3.1). The vertical axis relates to aspects of pupils' development, and the horizontal axis lists elements of learning. One can

Intellectual	Knowledge	Skills	Qualities
Physical			
Spiritual/religious			
Emotional/personal			
Social/moral			

FIGURE 3.1   A classification matrix of aims of education

remark the admixture of process and content aims – 'task' and 'achievement' conceptions of education. A similar matrix can be constructed out of the DES (1985b) conceptions of the organization of the curriculum (Figure 3.2).

What must be borne in mind when using these matrices is that they are essentially analytical models which are being used prescriptively (c.f. DES, 1985b). They do not describe actual channels of child development (Alexander, 1984) nor is any substantial justification for these conceptions proffered. In using them, then, the curriculum planner has to be aware that they do not reflect actual states of mind or lines of child development or curriculum plans, i.e. that development and education do not follow these discrete paths. The significance of this is to realize that they provide a helpful, if incomplete, framework for planners; they articulate the terms of the curriculum and educational debate. The framework must therefore

Areas of learning and experience \ Elements of learning	Knowledge	Concepts	Skills	Attitudes
Aesthetic and creative				
Human and social				
Linguistic and literary				
Mathematical				
Moral				
Physical				
Scientific				
Spiritual				
Technological				

FIGURE 3.2   Interpreting HMI classification of aims

be enabling and facilitating for planning rather than constricting or constraining; it must be a ladder rather than a cage.

The second important consideration for curriculum planners using these matrices is to ensure that every cell of the matrix is addressed. It is significant that in the Ashton, Kneen and Davies study (1975) there is an absence of 'skills' in the 'spiritual/religious' cell, and of 'knowledge' in the aesthetic development cell (c.f. Alexander, 1984); the question must be raised of the ideological taste betrayed by such omissions. If the models are to be used then perhaps they should be used in their entirety rather than partially.

In classifying aims the curriculum planner must ensure, then, that due weight is given to individual and societal needs, to comprehensiveness of coverage and expression; e.g. epistemological, ideological and psychological concerns, and to an articulation of the justification for the aims, the rationales on which they are premissed. Given that aims are fundamental building blocks of the curriculum, the values which underpin them must be thought through by curriculum planners and equally thoroughly expressed.

NATURE AND PURPOSE OF OBJECTIVES

In approaching the field of objectives, curriculum planners can define objectives as operational statements of the desired outcomes of curricula (c.f. Chapter 2). Tyler (1949) argues for the necessity of having objectives in curriculum planning and improvement in that

> if an educational program is to be planned and if efforts for continual improvement are to be made, it is very necessary to have some conception of the goals that are being aimed at. These educational objectives become the criteria by which materials are selected, content is outlined, instructional procedures are developed and tests and examinations are prepared.
>
> (Tyler, 1949, p.3)

Objectives, then, are far more specific and purportedly unambiguous than aims. They translate aims into practice coherently rather than haphazardly; they offer more precise direction than aims; aims are insufficient guides for making specific decisions about specific curricula. Aims orientate, they are strategical; objectives implement, they are tactical (c.f. Davies, 1976).

Objectives are operational in that they describe what the teacher or the child will be doing, they can prescribe outcomes in their statements of what the child or teacher should have achieved or practised or covered by the end of a lesson or course. An example of a lesson objective might be: 'the object of this lesson is for the children to learn the words and music of *Country Gardens'*, or 'the object of this lesson is to practise anaphoric and cataphoric reading cues in a piece of cloze procedure about hunting seals in the Arctic Circle'.

There are several claims for the purpose or value of planning the curriculum by objectives. Taba (1962), for example, suggests that they guide decisions on content selection and suitability of experiences to learn that content; they offer clarity in selecting from the vast areas of knowledge that which is necessary for the movement towards achieving aims; they clarify issues and thinking about purposes and intentions:

> the necessity for objectives is simply the necessity for us to know what it is we want children to learn if we are to be able to do our best to help them learn. Pupils must learn something, and how can we plan that they achieve that without being clear what it is.
>
> (Hirst, 1980, p.9)

The thrust of the argument here then is that objectives clarify thinking and clarify and specify pathways through knowledge. They enable curriculum planners to decide which ways are beneficial to the achievement of ends and purposes. There are many ways of learning a concept; for example, if one wished to learn about the concept of flotation one could learn practically by experimenting, vicariously by reading about it or by listening to a teacher talking about it, iconically (Bruner, 1960) by watching a film or video programme or by drawing a picture about it (c.f. Bruner in Chapter 1), or symbolically by writing about it. By being precise and specific in stating objectives, the curriculum planner can clarify the most apposite ways of attaining the objectives. Clarification, as has already been mentioned, is a critical quality of the reflective teacher.

Objectives facilitate evaluation, indeed they may predetermine evaluation criteria. Curriculum planners need to know their intentions for children's learning in order to judge how successfully the intentions have been achieved. It is quite ridiculous to argue that a course or a lesson went well if the criteria for that judgement were not clear; these criteria could be contained in the objectives. This has a twofold benefit: improvement of the curriculum is assisted if feedback on achievement is available and, second, it makes for better matching of tasks to children, setting realistic demands.

There are, however, problems with the notion of using objectives in the evaluation process, principally because they tend to lock evaluation into a certain mode — assessment and measurement rather than diagnosis and judgement. The problem is particularly acute in discussing behavioural objectives — to be reviewed later in the chapter.

The strongest justification for planning the curriculum by objectives lies in its appeal to rationality; that part of the meaning of an activity to be rational is that it should be directed to some clear goal or purpose. For the curriculum to be rational, then, it must state its purposes (Hirst, 1980):

> In curriculum decisions we are concerned with a programme of intentional, deliberately and consciously planned objectives...planned so that certain objectives will be reached, so that pupils will come to know certain things, have certain skills, will be able to appreciate certain things, have certain habits, patterns of emotional response and so on...curriculum activities are...the means to the intended ends.
>
> (Hirst, 1980, p.9)

Education, as mentioned earlier, is an intentional activity. Hirst (1975) argues that rational planning must adhere to Mill's principles of defining ends and then means to achieving them, and to Oakeshott's (1976a; 1976b) principle that curriculum planners must look to the specific activity, the specific school and the specific curriculum as practised in that school ('the idiom of the activity') to ascertain the most appropriate objectives. In this sense curriculum planning can scarcely ever be wholesale, but piecemeal (c.f. Skilbeck, 1984):

> all action takes place within a specific context and a set of traditions. It is only within this that rational development can take place. The idea of *ab initio*, *carte blanche* planning is a megalomaniac delusion....Rational planning is not, and cannot be Utopian. It must be piecemeal development on the spot, using all the available understanding and knowledge.
>
> (Hirst, 1975, pp. 14−15)

Hirst, then, offers a provocative reassertion of the need for objectives and indeed their usefulness for curriculum planners, cast in a powerful justificatory language.

Curriculum planning embraces general and specific objectives. An example of a general objective might be: 'to introduce children to scientific experimentation' or 'to interest pupils in local history', i.e. the setting out of a field of study. An example of a less general objective in this science field might read: 'the ability to apply various methods of separating and purifying chemicals to the demands of an astronaut's life support system in a space craft' (Whitfield, 1980, p. 86), or in fine art it might be: 'to develop skill in mixing water colour' (ibid., p. 25). At a highly specific level it could be: 'to measure in kilometres per hour (kph) the speed of an articulated lorry travelling down Nonesuch hill with a full load', where an explicit task is set, the conditions in which that task is performed are clearly delineated (travelling downhill with a full load) and the criteria for successful performance indicated (measuring speed in kph).

The issue raised by different levels of objectives is significant, for it directs attention to the point that though objectives are more specific than aims, being operational, they are not necessarily solely highly specific ends written in narrow behavioural terms. Such recognition brings out the view that objectives can be short-term or long-term, though in reality argument tends to treat them as shorter rather than longer term ends. With this in mind it is possible to present a model showing how objectives are devised and who devises them (Figure 3.3).

The model is perhaps descriptive; its prescriptivity is highly questionable. The caution that must be exercised in examining this model concerns the discreteness of each level and type of decisions on objectives and courses, for it could be argued (Carson, 1984) that decisions on general aims and curriculum areas are not the preserve of the DES, LEA, or senior management levels of schools. In fact, for primary schools the opposite may be more pertinent. The danger of this model lies in the way that it might be seen to prescribe a bureaucratic, hierarchical structure of curriculum planning rather than a democratic, open structure. An alternative then could be presented (Figure 3.4).

In this model the concept of negotiation and interaction is presented, again requiring reflective thinking about education and the curriculum by teachers. It accords with professional autonomy and its concomitant responsibility to all major participants in the curriculum planning process. Teachers are agents in planning rather than simply recipients of others' plans.

General	Bodies	Form of objectives	Decisions on courses
Level 1 ↓	DES LEA	Very generalized	Major areas of the curriculum defined
Level 2 ↓	School or department	Broad parameters and direction	Decisions on the framing of courses
Level 3 ↓	Teams of staff	More detailed objectives	Course content and sequence as a whole
Level 4 ↓ Specific	Teacher	Highly specific behaviours and content	Lesson content

FIGURE 3.3 The range of curriculum objectives presented by levels of decision-makers

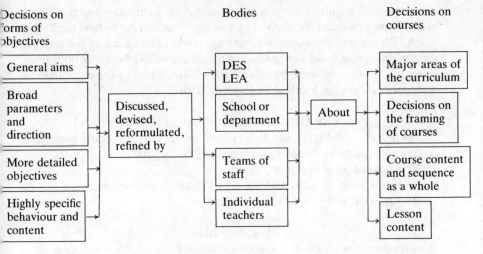

FIGURE 3.4 A model of participatory decision-making in objectives-based planning

CLASSIFYING OBJECTIVES

Objectives need not simply be classified in terms of levels of generality — from general to specific, as mentioned in the previous section. What is required here is an analysis of types of objectives so that curriculum planners can identify scope for balance, coverage and breadth in planning. One useful form of classification finds five sorts of objectives (Taba, 1962):

1. Objectives concerning knowledge (facts, ideas, principles, concepts).
2. Objectives concerning reflective thinking (critical thinking, interpreting data, applying facts and principles, logical reasoning).
3. Objectives concerning values and attitudes.
4. Objectives concerning sensitivities and feelings.
5. Objectives concerning skills.

This has clear resonances with Scrimshaw's (1983) categorization of components of children's learning, outlined in Chapter 2. Alternatively, a much publicized way of classifying objectives is taxonomically. Bloom and his associates (1956) developed taxonomies of educational objectives, specifying levels of generality and specificity, higher and lower order objectives. They intended to cover three domains: cognitive, affective and psychomotor — the head, the heart and the hand (Kelly, 1982). The taxonomy of cognitive objectives appeared in 1956; Krathwohl, Bloom and Masia produced the second taxonomy − of affective objectives − in 1956. Bloom and his associates were somewhat dismissive of the psychomotor domain and did not produce a taxonomy of psychomotor objectives; instead, it was devised by Harrow (1984). The cognitive domain is categorized into six levels thus (Bloom, 1956):

Level one (the most specific and lowest order)
Knowledge − ability to recall specifics, universals, methods, processes, patterns, structures or settings (Bloom, 1956, p. 201).
1.10 Knowledge of specifics.
1.20 Knowledge of ways and means of dealing with specifics.
1.30 Knowledge of universals in a field.

Level two
Comprehension − which requires knowledge, an ability to grasp what is being communicated, to be able to use the material or idea without necessarily relating it to other material or seeing its fullest implications, (ibid., p. 204).
2.10 Translation.
2.20 Interpretation.
2.30 Extrapolation.

Level three
Application − which requires knowledge and comprehension, an ability to use ideas, concepts or principles in particular and concrete situations (ibid., p. 205).

Level four
Analysis − which subsumes levels one to three, an ability to break down an idea or concept into its constituents parts and their interrelationship which clarify or illuminate the whole curriculum (ibid., p. 205).
4.10 Analysis of elements.
4.20 Analysis of relationships.
4.30 Analysis of organizational principles.

Level five
Synthesis − which subsumes levels one to four, an ability to assemble elements into a unified whole not clearly present initially (ibid., p. 206).
5.10 Production of unique communication.
5.20 Production of a plan or a proposed set of relations.
5.30 Derivation of a set of abstract relations.

Level six

[Evaluation] – which subsumes levels one to five, an ability to appropriate criteria to judge the value of material and methods for given purposes (ibid., p. 207).
6.10 Judgement in terms of internal evidence.
6.20 Judgement in terms of external criteria.

An example of a low-order objective might be: 'to list five types of defences for castles', whereas a high-order objective might be: 'to say why castle defence "x" is the most effective'. Low-order objectives make slight cognitive demand, e.g. 'to add two and two', 'to weigh five buckets of dry sand'; whereas high-order objectives involve applying many concepts and abstractions, e.g. 'to suggest why *The Shrinking of Treehorn* is a good book', or 'to appreciate the icy atmosphere depicted in Vaughan Williams's *Sinfonia Antarctica*'. One can construct a chart to graph the twin continua of low to high order and specific to general objectives (Figure 3.5).

An example of a low-order, general objective (the top left-hand quadrant) might be: 'to know that many trees shed their leaves in autumn'. The significant phrase here is 'know that' – a fact, rather than 'knowing how' – an understanding (see Chapter 1).

Examples of high-order, general objectives (the top right-hand quadrant) might be: 'to understand the principles of capitalism', or 'to appreciate the need for ecological interdependence', where both understanding and a valuative perspective on that understanding are required. An example of a low-order, specific objective (the bottom left-hand quadrant) might read: 'to colour in three printed houses'; whereas examples of high-order, specific objectives might be: 'to write a critical commentary on *The Wild Swans of Coole*', or 'to appreciate the need for vitamins in the human body'.

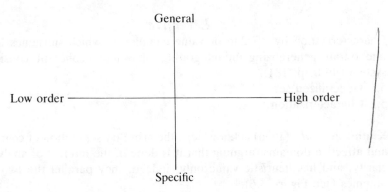

FIGURE 3.5 Two dimensions of curriculum objectives

In the affective domain five levels are identified:

Level one

Receiving – attending to, being sensitized to the existence of certain phenomena and stimuli (Krathwohl *et al.*, 1956, p. 176).

1.1 Awareness.
1.2 Willingness to receive.
1.3 Controlled or selected attention.

Level two

Responding – which subsumes level one, actively attending and interested (ibid., p. 178).

2.1 Acquiescense in responding.
2.2 Willingness to respond.
2.3 Satisfaction in response.

Level three

Valuing – which subsumes levels one and two, judging worth and internalizing values, developing conscience (ibid., p. 180).

3.1 Acceptance of a value.
3.2 Preference for a value.
3.3 Commitment (conviction).

Level four

Organization – which subsumes levels one to three, organizing and adapting values, determining their interrelationships and prioritizing them (ibid., p. 182).

4.1 Conceptualization of a value.
4.2 Organization of a value system.

Level five

Characterization by a value or value complex – which subsumes levels one to four, generalizing and integrating values into a coherent, consistent system (ibid., p. 184).

5.1 Generalized set.
5.2 Characterization.

Krathwohl *et al.*, (1956) acknowledge the arbitrary separation of cognitive and affective domains, arguing that it is done in the interest of analytical clarity, and has heuristic value only; indeed, they parallel the two taxonomies (see Figure 3.6).

Cognitive domain	Affective domain
knowledge	receiving
comprehension	responding
application	valuing
analysis	conceptualization
synthesis	conceptualization
evaluation	organization and characterization

FIGURE 3.6 Matching two taxonomies

In the psychomotor domain, Harrow (1974) delineates four levels of behaviour:

Level one

Observing – where the child observes the techniques and processes of a behaviour.

Level two

Imitating – which subsumes level one, where the child practises and performs given movements cautiously.

Level three

Practising – subsuming levels one and two, where movements become habitual, unconscious and smooth.

Level four

Adapting – subsuming levels one to three, where the child adapts routines and processes to suit her or his own purposes.

The claimed advantages of using taxonomies for devising curriculum objectives lie in their hierarchical classification systems and their clarity (Cave, 1971). They offer curriculum planners a checklist for achieving comprehensiveness in the curriculum (Bloom, 1956), knowing which domain and level of the curriculum assists analysis and coverage of the curriculum. Second, they facilitate communication of intentions and purposes between curriculum planners by offering a common referent. Third, they assist in pitching test items at an appropriate level and are useful for evaluation purposes. Fourth, it is claimed that they should stimulate thought about educational problems. Finally, their authors contend that the taxonomic approach is seen as a useful and effective tool for devising objectives.

Against these points are arranged several powerful arguments. It is suggested (Sockett, 1976) that Bloom's taxonomies demonstrate a lack of epistemological coherence, assuming that different areas of understanding and learning will have a similar structure; for example, that the structuring of aesthetic understandings will be similar to the structuring of understandings in the physical sciences, or maths or morals, or that problem-solving in mathematics will be the same as problem-solving in physics, or art, or music.

Just as the taxonomies artificially separate behaviours into domains, a fact which is acknowledged by the compilers (Krathwohl *et al.*, 1956), so within each taxonomy behaviour is separated artificially. For example, knowledge entails comprehension, recall and application simultaneously; knowledge does not equate solely with recall.

The thrust of this criticism is twofold. It acknowledges the undesirability of attempting to categorize behaviour too tightly as this reflects poorly the actuality of both epistemology and the learning child; behaviours cannot be pigeon-holed into single, discrete units. There is a suggestion in the compilation of the taxonomies that, even though each successive level subsumes the lower levels, there is no clear or immediate relationship between levels (Davies, 1976), which is epistemologically fallacious.

The second implication of attempting to separate behaviours for which taxonomies have been criticized (Hirst, 1975) is that they reduce the complexity of the curriculum and of learning to a level of simplicity which renders them both meaningless and fruitless, neglecting the complex interrelationships of skills, concepts, values, attitudes and perceptions (Hirst, 1975). The effort required to do justice to that complexity would be both time-consuming and, from the preceding argument, wasted.

As a model for primary curriculum planning, which celebrates unity of knowledge and experiences, the taxonomic approach, which separates behaviours rather than integrates them, is perhaps inappropriate. One can nevertheless look to taxonomies not necessarily as they have been interpreted, but as they were intended to be used – as tools to stimulate thought (Bloom, 1956) – however flawed or incomplete they may be, a fact acknowledged by their authors. If they serve to promote discussion, debate, reflective thinking and teaching, then there must surely be a place for them in the curriculum planner's repertoire. One has to remark on the considerable currency commanded by taxonomic approaches to devising curricula: witness the Barrett taxonomy of reading comprehension (1972) and the hostility provoked to taxonomic planning (c.f. Smith, 1971; Morrison, 1984), to realize that as conceptual aids to debate they are perhaps useful.

Objectives have been classified according to Taba's (1962) scheme and to taxonomic schemes initiated by Bloom and others. A third classification exists which sorts objectives into types, principally three:

1. Specific statements of intent.
2. Behavioural objectives.
3. Expressive objectives.

The first of these has already been discussed, the others will be discussed in order.

BEHAVIOURAL OBJECTIVES

Behavioural objectives − sometimes called instructional objectives − are statements which prescribe the behavioural outcomes of a program. They specify intended learner or learned behaviour as a result of a lesson or course; these behaviours are observable and measurable (Tyler, 1949). For an objective to be behavioural it must satisfy three conditions (Mager, 1962):

1. It must identify intended terminal behaviour which demonstrates that learning has taken place.
2. It must describe the important conditions under which that behaviour is to occur.
3. It must specify the criteria of acceptable performance.

Wiles and Bondi (1984) name this the ABCD rule: the behavioural objective specifies the Audience of the objective (who will be displaying the behaviour); the Behaviour which will be displayed (the task); the condition, the Context of the behaviour (what material or resources will be used); the Degree of completion, how the performance of the behaviour will be assessed, what the criteria are for successful performance.

An example of a behavioural objective which fulfils the ABCD rule would be: 'at the end of this lesson the children will be able to draw a dinosaur on stiff card and cut it out carefully'. Here:

A = the children
B = drawing a dinosaur and cutting it out
C = on stiff card
D = carefully

Another example would be: 'by the end of the lesson the children will have successfully made a ten-page booklet which illustrates seventeenth century clothing fashions in England'. Here:

A = the children
B = making a book illustrating seventeenth century English clothing fashions
C = a ten-page booklet
D = successfully made

Significantly, then, the behavioural objective must specify both the content and the process (Tyler, 1949): the knowledge and information and how it is to be acquired, utilized or practised; what it is and what will be done with it. Clearly, the success of a behavioural objective lies in its ability to describe a behaviour explicitly and unambiguously.

Fashions dictate the support or resistance offered to behavioural objectives, and there are significant arguments for and against their use. Interestingly, many arguments advanced in their favour are also used against them, revealing the ideological bases and conflicts in the debate. In their support are ranked several important considerations. They can be claimed to constitute the most fully worked out expression of rational planning outlined earlier, and have a curriculum pedigree which can be traced back to the early part of the century (Bobbitt, 1918; Charters, 1924). They have internal consistency with major models of curriculum planning (Tyler, 1949; Taba, 1962; Wheeler, 1967).

Such a pedigree claims the respectability of the behavioural tradition and scientific methodology employed in earlier curriculum writings. In this view their predetermination of children's terminal behaviour is seen as a merit. It is claimed that they facilitate curriculum organization in a means-end style by focusing many variables and problems into a chronologically linear sequence. On a practical level they can clarify thinking and resolve ambiguities (Popham, 1975), exposing the trivial and yet enabling planning in detail to be promoted. As with arguments in favour of taxonomic detailing of objectives, so in behavioural objectives a strength is claimed in their communicability to teachers and, importantly, to learners, reducing learner anxiety about the future and the requirements laid on them.

From a conservative ideology they can be said to concern the acquisition of the 'known' — a received curriculum — the corollary of which is to cast the teacher into the role of an expert or controller. This can be extended beyond the teacher's control to suggest that curriculum planners beginning from a statement of behavioural objectives can produce 'teacher-proof' materials and curricula, with instructions, goals or objectives so unambiguously formulated as to render teacher intervention or modification unnecessary. The teacher simply carries out the prescriptions.

This is seen positively as a means of supporting anxious teachers and ensuring that a sound education is provided even by inadequate teachers. At the level of evaluation it is claimed that behavioural objectives lead logically to evaluation, suggesting explicitly what has to be evaluated and the criteria for that evaluation, i.e. that evaluation is meaningful rather than being an imposed evaluation which may not be completely relevant (for example, nationally standardized tests of performance). Being measurable and testable in behaviour, behavioural objectives are useful fuel in the accountability debate.

Against these arguments are several key questions and doubts, many of which express the uncertainty of using behavioural objectives as the basis for planning the curriculum in general, and the primary curriculum in particular, notably their incompatability with the primary ethos set out at the end of Chapter 1. Arguments against the use of behavioural objectives present themselves at various levels. At an ideological level the notion of behaviourism is suspect in that it supports an instrumental or utilitarian view of education rather than regarding education as intrinsically worthwhile. This casts learners in a very passive, accepting role rather than as agents of their own learning – a view on which the primary ethos is predicated. Similarly, it casts teachers in given roles as experts, managers, technicians and controllers rather than co-learners, guides, chairpersons, facilitators, catalysts, denying perhaps their autonomy (Pring, 1973), their agency (Giroux, 1983). Such a view restricts the fluidity and breadth of teacher–pupil interaction and relationships which is one of the cornerstones of the primary ethos.

In this light the development of 'teacher-proof' materials is a weakness, a disadvantage rather than a strength. The concept of education supported by behavioural objectives suggests fixity and certainty whereas the concept of education espoused at the end of Chapter 1 suggests unpredictable outcomes (Stenhouse, 1975). The process of education is replaced by output dependence. That output might well be a set of unconnected skills rather than an uneducated person. In this vein MacDonald-Ross (1975) contends that behavioural objectives are constricting in the sense of neglecting the value of 'voyages of exploration' – opportunistic learning and teaching, shared discovery learning, the unanticipated class events and interests – this despite Popham's (1975) assertion that opportunism is to be welcomed as long as it contributes to the attainment of worthwhile objectives, and Pope's (1983) assertion that teachers embarking on 'voyages of exploration' should have clearly addressed the question of accountability for their actions.

In sympathy with this approach, James (1968) argues that using objectives does not ensure understanding; children may go through the motions of an activity without really understanding it. In the primary curriculum, as with the curriculum of the later years, the emphasis on understanding renders this criticism noteworthy. A critical educational and ideological argument against behaviourism is advanced by Hirst (1975), who holds that the central features of education (internalized processes, thoughts, values) are not reducible to the observable states which behavioural objectives require to be demonstrated, i.e. that behaviourism at root is an inappropriate conception of education (MacDonald-Ross, 1975; Stenhouse, 1975).

At an epistemological level, it is argued that behavioural objectives mistake the nature of knowledge, seeing it as purely in a product version, rather than product and process together. Thus it leans towards a 'facts'-based curriculum which may be acceptable to conservative ideologies, but which unfairly represents the central tenets of the primary ethos which are founded on empiricist views as well as rationalist views of knowledge.

At a curriculum level behavioural objectives, it is suggested, are unsuitable for vast areas of the curriculum. For example, in science the principle of falsifiability is violated if outcomes are specified (Sockett, 1976), in the humanities and aesthetic education important outcomes, e.g. appreciation, are pushed aside (Eisner, 1975). Eisner suggests that it is not possible to prespecify outcomes of appreciation except at the level of banality; that it is undesirable to specify the content of appreciation, indeed using behavioural objectives could easily diminish creativity. Eisner is arguing that the subject matter of education necessarily affects the applicability of planning by behavioural objectives – that whereas they may be useful in planning for highly specific skills to be trained, e.g. stripping down a car engine, or 'handwriting', they are unsuitable for areas of the curriculum which do not fit comfortably into being so tightly specified; major areas of the curriculum are not susceptible to planning by this form of objectives. Behavioural objectives predetermine only one pathway through curricular knowledge (MacDonald-Ross, 1975) which may be inappropriate for many areas of the curriculum and many learners (though Pope, 1983, offers a rejoinder to this, commenting that some paths through knowledge are less effective than others and that in the interests of economic teaching efforts must be made to establish those ways which are most effective).

At a practical level there are several inadequacies in planning by behavioural objectives. As with taxonomies, so behavioural objectives miss the complexity of the curriculum; the ramifications of this are several. Either curriculum planners have to amass an inordinately long and unworkable list of objectives (MacDonald-Ross, 1975) to do justice to the complexity of the curriculum, or they concern themselves with that which can be easily expressed and operationalized. If one opts for the former then, apart from the considerable time needed to write lengthy lists of unambiguous objectives, there is no guarantee that teachers will either refer to them (Taylor, 1970) or in fact need to refer to them. Witness the neglect of the pages of objectives reproduced at the end of every *Science 5-13* book; teachers teach efficiently without them, and there is little reason to suspect that inattention to behavioural objectives has been detrimental to their teaching (Stenhouse, 1975).

If one opts for the latter then teachers may well be dealing only in trivial and low-level processes. Popham (1975) would argue that a measure of this is acceptable, for in exposing the trivial the planner can see more clearly the significant issues, and plan those more carefully.

This is perhaps a slur on the expertise of teachers as planners. It also presupposes that behavioural objectives can be written in unambiguous terms, which is questionable (MacDonald-Ross, 1975; Sockett, 1976) as words themselves have different meanings according to contexts and users' frames of reference. For example, what is unambiguous to one person may be ambiguous or unintelligible to a child or another person. Even acknowledging Pope's (1983) valid point that difficulty in reducing ambiguity may be due to lack of clarity in the planner's mind, it nevertheless remains a serious problem which semantic analysis exacerbates rather than solves. At a practical level the argument that behavioural objectives are necessary for clear evaluation is fictitious; one might require objectives, certainly, but these need not be behaviourally expressed. Similarly, casting evaluation at the end of an educational program presupposes only a terminal, summative form of evaluation, whereas perhaps evaluation should be continual and formative. It also presupposes a particular form of terminal evaluation — achievement measurement — which is limiting and perhaps ideologically unsuited to the primary ethos.

Finally, at a curriculum development level, behavioural objectives offer little guidance to planners, for they do not address the question of the origin of the objectives. This renders their claimed value of neutrality a weakness rather than a strength. They presuppose, perhaps, consensus where there is conflict over moral choices about aims and goals. Unless curriculum planners are apprised of aims and values upon which the behavioural objectives are based, there can be little useful discourse about new directions in curriculum planning. The results of such neglect could be an inability to take forward the curriculum to match societal and cultural change; it would present a static rather than regenerative curriculum.

Thus the picture of behavioural objectives is cloudy; the curriculum planner, while conceding that there are times when they may be useful, has to recognize their limitations and the difficulty of writing them. Are they so difficult to write that only 'experts' can devise them – in which case they can be a dangerous tool in curriculum direction and control, or should teachers be versed in their devising and utilization?

EXPRESSIVE OBJECTIVES

Expressive objectives can be seen as an attempt to preserve a measure of rigour in curriculum planning but to avoid the unpalatable excesses of the behavioural objectives model. They derive from Eisner (1975); their purpose is to describe learning situations which are intended to evoke personal responses from pupils rather than prespecifying a specific or uniform response or outcome. Hence their expression is gentler than that of behavioural objectives. They specify an activity, experience or encounter in which learners engage but draw back from specifying an intended learning outcome; they are evocative rather than prescriptive. Examples of expressive objectives might be: 'to visit a church and discuss what was interesting' or 'to depict, in any medium, the story of Rama and Sita'.

One can detect in expressive objectives three key features. First, they are apposite in planning in the aesthetic and humanities areas of the curriculum, where a personal response is a central aim. Second, by dint of that intention to evince a personal response, they are necessarily open-ended; they focus on processes as well as content. This is in keeping with the primary ethos of Chapter 1. Third, they refer directly to the classroom learning model outlined in Chapter 2, where the key features – experience, observation, transformation, communication, incubation and accommodation – are key features also of expressive objectives. That model is premissed on the primary ethos. The intention of expressive objectives is to seek diversity rather than homogeneity of response, uniqueness rather than similarity; this accords well with the central features of progressive ideology.

EVALUATING AIMS AND OBJECTIVES

In evaluating aims and objectives, curriculum planners may address a range of questions which seek to examine their place and usefulness in building the curriculum:

- How worthwhile are the aims and objectives?
- How well and how comprehensively do the aims reflect the philo-

sophies, contexts of and constraints on the curriculum and its planning?

- What are the ideological commitments of these aims and objectives?
- How clearly do the objectives follow from the aims?
- How well and how comprehensively do the objectives serve the aims?
- How practical and practicable are the objectives?
- How well do the objectives express different levels of cognitive, affective and psychomotor demand?
- How far do the objectives steer a middle course between necessary and unnecessary specificity?
- How are the aims and objectives decided, and by whom?
- How completely do the objectives address knowledge, concepts, skills, qualities, attitudes, personal and social development?
- How can taxonomies be used effectively in curriculum planning?
- How clearly stated are the aims and objectives?
- How appropriate are the aims and objectives to the children's individual needs, interests and abilities?
- How can these objectives be developed and formulated?
- What alterations to existing philosophies, practices, organizations and managements are suggested by aims for a new piece of the planned curriculum?
- How will these aims and objectives assist in planning content, pedagogy and evaluation?
- How appropriate is the differentiation of aims and objectives in planning?
- How well do the aims and objectives cover issues which permeate the curriculum e.g. multicultural education, equal opportunities, health education, information technology, political education?
- How will aims and objectives for the curriculum be discussed, negotiated and decided?
- How will disagreement on the formulation and the content of the aims and objectives be managed?
- Who will decide the aims and objectives?

While the list is by no means exhaustive, it attempts to draw together the range of issues raised through the book so far. This involves looking at the stages and levels of curriculum planning, the managerial aspects of the curriculum debate and the structuring of the curriculum. Aims and objectives should embody and reflect such a range. Discussion of aims and objectives is ongoing just as the curriculum debate is never static.

CONCLUSION

In conclusion there are four main points which merit attention by curriculum planners considering aims and objectives. First, despite the many and significant problems associated with the employment of behavioural objectives, they need not necessarily be totally disregarded in planning the curriculum. Skilbeck (1984) offers a strong argument for their retention, suggesting that curriculum planning ought to attempt to identify desirable and desired learning outcomes in children, that the implausibility and undesirability of predicting outcomes in certain curriculum areas should not blind planners to the need for anticipating outcomes in others.

Second, if it is accepted that objectives need not be behavioural, then there remains a very powerul argument in favour of teachers planning by objectives (Hirst, 1980), that using objectives does not necessarily mean predicting highly specific outcomes. If knowledge is tentative and provisional then the objective can be written to reflect and incorporate this. This reduces the need to regard objectives as having to conform to taxonomic structures (Hirst, 1975); taxonomies are tools for thought, not necessarily prescriptive guidelines. Third, linked to this is the notion that objectives cover a wide field – knowledge, products, processes, concepts, skills, attitudes and values, organizations, activities and experiences (c.f. Carter and Hooley, 1983). Which type of objective curriculum planners may use is determined by ideology, epistemology, psychology, cultural and sociological pressures and constraints.

This issue of appropriacy engages the final point of fundamentally questioning the desirability of objectives. While one might accept the need for, and the desirability of, expressing aims and very general objectives and goals, it is the thin end of a wedge whose predetermining force at the specific and detailed end of curriculum planning is to stultify development and curriculum change, to minimize teacher and pupil autonomy, and to foreswear commitment to the ethos of primary education. Between these poles of commitment and abandonment of aims and detailed prescriptive objectives there is ample room for manoeuvre by curriculum planners.

4
SETTING THE
CLASSROOM ENVIRONMENT

In the process of applying planning models to the curriculum as experienced by the children and staff, the effects of the relationships between the primary ethos, constraints on the curriculum, and aims, goals and objectives have begun to be sketched. These have so far remained at a level of generality or abstraction which curriculum planners certainly need but which are incomplete without more specific reference to the diverse classroom organizations and children's learning which obtain in primary schools.

This chapter, then, moves the discussion on to examining this diversity. While acknowledging certain constraints on schooling it is hoped here that by raising the issues that key classroom variables are changeable, the notion of the earlier chapters (that the curriculum in its widest sense is negotiable) will be maintained and be seen to be operating at the different levels outlined in previous chapters – contextual, managerial, conceptual, strategic and tactical. It has already been suggested in discussing the primary ethos that the classroom should be a highly charged environment designed to accelerate learning; some of its characteristics have been listed previously. What are the classroom day-to-day elements which are open to modification? In this chapter, six such elements are highlighted: pedagogy and organization of children's learning, time, space, materials, children and the classroom ethos. The chapter thus acts as a bridge between the theoretical and contextual issues outlined in the earlier chapters and the practical world of everyday classroom life. It serves to raise questions which evaluators of that everyday life and the planning for it will have to address.

PEDAGOGY

While pedagogy has been the recipient of frequent conceptions, categorizations and typifications (e.g. CACE, 1967; Bennett, 1976; Galton, Simon and Croll, 1980; Bennett *et al.*, 1984), the threads which unite them all have been the twin urges to classify teaching in terms of ideological and product criteria. Pejorative overtones surround the efficacy of the alleged polar extremes of child-centred and traditional or formal approaches (Cox and Dyson, 1971; Boyson and Cox, 1975; Callaghan, 1976). The mutually exclusive nature of this dichotomy has been challenged at a theoretical level (Morrison, 1985; 1986a), while Bennett (1976) attempted to show the middle ground between them at a practical level.

It is assumed perhaps that characteristics or indicators of teaching styles can be identified. The reality of this situation is cloudier. It would be foolish to locate a specific pedagogical practice solely in one ideological, epistemological or psychological tradition; indeed, the same practice can serve a spectrum of values and intentions. Rather, the notion of typifying teaching and learning styles should be used as a tool to promote reflective thinking on the appropriacy of the pedagogy to the task, the learner and the teacher. The primary class teacher does not adhere rigidly to one set of pedagogical principles (Galton *et al.*, 1980), nor does deviation from one or two styles necessarily indicate a shift of ideology (see Chapter 1). However, given a commitment to a particular ideological standpoint, one can of course delineate a group of practices which may serve it more appropriately than another group. Further, one can suggest considerations and problems which have to be addressed if the success of those practices is to be maximized. This is the concern here; rather than offering typifications, the focus is on pedagogies which serve the elements of the primary ethos outlined in Chapter 1.

To portray the scope of these pedagogies for initial convenience a continuum can be set up from a teacher-centred, didactic and perhaps vicarious approach, through group work, to individual heuristic modes of classroom experience and learning. This perhaps serves the caution which must be exercised in falsely presuming that didactic approaches may not suit individual children's needs or that heuristic approaches alone meet the demands of child-centred education. If liberalism is one of the tenets of primary education then eclectic use of pedagogies must follow in its wake.

Translating these theoretical issues of primary pedagogy into practice takes the curriculum planner into discussing and evaluating the nature and purpose of group work, integrated and semi-integrated day organizations, and open-plan schooling.

GROUP WORK

The end of Chapter 1 cited the value of peer group support and an enriching social atmosphere as two central characteristics of the primary school ethos. In approaching group work one can itemize the claimed advantages of such an organizational principle and observe how they are rooted in the best elements by primary school teaching and learning. They demonstrate an epistemological commitment to both processes and products, and an ideological affinity to child-centred education, with its psychological support from notions of meeting children's needs by an appropriate variety of pedagogical styles. It is claimed for group work (CACE, 1967; Yeomans, 1983) that it:

- Helps pupils to work co-operatively.
- Allows children to learn from each other.
- Encourages the involvement of apathetic children.
- Removes the stigma of failure from certain pupils.
- Affords teachers the opportunity to circulate.
- Affords children the opportunity to work at their own pace.
- Allows children to respect each others' strengths and weaknesses.
- Allows children more access to equipment which is in short supply.
- Enables joint goals and planning to be established.
- Enables children to see each other as an important resource.
- Encourages a friendly atmosphere in the group through social talk.
- Facilitates mixed ability teaching.
- Facilitates the integrated day.
- Encourages joint decision-making.
- Affords opportunities for the development of leadership in children.
- Stimulates the development of children's autonomy.
- Facilitates the teaching of vertically grouped children.
- Is a valuable experience in itself, focusing on processes of learning as well as products.
- Fosters resourcefulness in children through a minimum of teacher direction.
- Enables children to explore and handle ideas.

- Promotes personal and social development, self-esteem and self-confidence.
- Promotes high- and low-order thinking.
- Encourages children to express themselves freely and clearly.
- Promotes mutual integration of children in multi-ethnic classes.
- Encourages a positive attitude to school.
- Encourages children to engage in the problem of disagreement.
- Improves discussion and classroom talk through:
    - (a) initiating discussion of a new issue;
    - (b) qualifying another person's contribution;
    - (c) implicitly accepting a qualification;
    - (d) extending a previous qualification;
    - (e) asking for an illustration to test a generalization;
    - (f) providing an example;
    - (g) using evidence to challenge an assertion;
    - (h) reformulating one's own previous assertion;
    - (i) obtaining information from others;
    - (j) completing unfinished utterances;
    - (k) encouraging others to continue;
    - (l) inviting others to continue;
    - (m) repeating with modifications;
    - (n) supporting another's assertion with evidence.

Evaluation could be undertaken to see how well the claims made for group work are being achieved. It must be acknowledged that the notion of a group is ambiguous. The teacher can have children sitting in groups but actually engaged in individual work (Galton *et al.*, 1980). A group describes a collaborative enterprise rather than a seating arrangement; children contributing to the common task. However, while this is clearly true it does not fully conceptualize group work, for the teacher can hold the notion of a group in her or his mind even though a collaborative piece of work is not being undertaken. Common examples of the 'group in the mind' are where the teacher notes which children are at a similar stage in mathematics or language work. The notion of a group here is used as a categorial device for monitoring the progression of children. The thrust of this section, however, is to consider the idea of group work as children actually working together co-operatively on a single project.

If one accepts this latter interpretation then the teacher is faced with crucial decisions in implementing this pedagogic style:

1. What are the criteria for grouping children?
   (a) Age;
   (b) Ability;

    (c) Friendship;
    (d) Interest in the task;
    (e) Pupils' preferred learning styles;
    (f) Stage of work;
    (g) Focus of task.
2. What is the optimum size of the group? How will this be decided?
3. Who decides on the size and composition of the group?
4. How permanent is the grouping? Is it on an *ad hoc* basis?
5. Does the focus of the task really lend itself to group work? Is there sufficient 'mileage' in the work? Are the tasks realistic?
6. What timing considerations must be given to group work?
    (a) Time(s) of the day in which group work is done;
    (b) How long the group work sessions will last;
    (c) How much of a total session will be done in groups.
7. How will each group be organized?
    (a) Leaders;
    (b) Division of labour;
    (c) Reporter.
8. What are the roles of the teacher in group work?
    (a) Catalyst;
    (b) Facilitator;
    (c) Consultant:
    (d) Discipline agent;
    (e) Director;
    (f) Clarifier;
    (g) Setter of standards (quality and quantity);
    (h) Instructor;
    (i) Questioner;
    (j) Setter of social climate;
    (k) Organizer;
    (l) Provider of resources;
    (m) Monitor, keeping pupils on task.
9. What is the nature of teacher intervention in group work?
10. What changes are necessary in the teachers' role perceptions of themselves and their children if children's autonomy and choice are necessary components?

On a practical level there are problematic areas which need to be resolved before embarking on group work:

1. How to begin and end group sessions; how to instruct children to go into groups and begin working.
2. How to sum up, reinforce and follow up group sessions.

3. What to do if children do not want to work with each other.
4. What to do if a child disagrees with a group decision.
5. What to do if children are not interested and not co-operating.
6. How to ensure match with individual needs.
7. How to evaluate what is happening in the group.
8. How to record a child's achievement/progress/contribution in a group enterprise.
9. How to evaluate the group or individual.
10. How to have groups report back or provide feedback on the results of their work.
11. How to ensure that each child knows what is expected of her or him.

Evaluation of group work could usefully address these questions.

The problems facing curriculum planners and teachers, particularly new teachers, are those of beginning to undertake the task of moving a class of children who perhaps are unused to working in groups towards this form of learning style. At a simplistic level a stage model can be suggested:

Stage one
Have only one or two groups working apart from the class at any one time while the remainder of the class is involved in class or individually based work.

Stage two
Each group replicates the same activity.

Stage three
Each group works on the same activity or focus in a variety of ways.

Stage four
Each group works on a variety of aspects of a topic or focus, one aspect per group.

Stage five
Each group works on a variety of aspects of a topic or focus, covering many key aspects; children do the planning.

Stage six
Each group works on one aspect of a variety of activities

Stage seven
Each group works on aspects of a variety of topics or foci.

Clearly, the size and composition of the groups is a critical factor in their success, an over-ambitious move to group work could well be a recipe for difficulty. The key to the problem perhaps is the notion of flexibility, the groups can be of varying sizes and permanence to suit the task, the children and the teacher. With fluid groupings a 'rolling programme' can be adopted to obviate the problem of beginning many groups simultaneously. As children finish on the 'rolling programme' so they can be set away on another activity which may be in groups or individually. Thus the notion of children working at different rates is used as an organizational strength rather than as a source of difficulty and endless interruption to the teacher.

THE INTEGRATED DAY

Moving from extended use of group work facilitates the introduction of the integrated day. The term is an umbrella phrase for a variety of practices (Brown and Precious, 1968), for example:

- Numerous activities occurring at the same time, directed by the teacher.
- Children working at different tasks in the same subject area.
- Rotating groups for organization.
- Numerous activities occurring at the same time, pupils deciding the order – the assignment system.
- Directed work in the morning, freedom of choice in the afternoon.
- Teacher structures the learning situations, children choose the activity.
- Children choose their activity for a set time each week.

If one asks 'what has to be integrated?' then it is possible to see that at the heart of notions of this form of organization lies a set of beliefs which accord strongly with the primary ethos outlined at the end of Chapter 1 (see also Brogden, 1983). On an epistemological level it lends itself to both integrated views of knowledge and to the learning of both processes and products, where the child integrates the diverse elements of school experiences individualistically and in a way which facilitates the preservation of the 'whole' personality and which fosters autonomous learning. From an ideological and psychological perspective, it meets the core tenets of child-centred ideology in a way which does not preclude attention to content, products and external demands on the school curriculum.

Further, one can itemize the strengths of its claims thus, that it:

- Allows individualized learning in content and pace, which makes for greater child involvement and interest.
- Uses teacher time very efficiently.
- Promotes children's autonomy.
- Allows teachers to cater for different rates of learning.
- Increases children's motivation by promoting and utilizing children's choice.
- Caters for flexible learning styles.
- Increases the likelihood of children interacting with their environment.
- Facilitates vertical grouping.

Given this ambitious set of claims, the organizational implications are several. Attention has to be given to: grouping; span of children's attention; timing and pacing of the changeover from one activity to another; change of physical position (how long children can remain in one place); limitation of movement; even use of room space to minimize disturbance; how to plan the work of individuals and groups; how to record the progress and content of children and their work; how to allocate assignments to groups; how to introduce new resources to groups; how to make optimum use of the teacher; what classroom layout is most effective.

Such considerations require that with children who are unused to working this system, as with any innovation, the golden rule is to progress in manageable stages to a fully integrated system. Moves to total integration can be charted thus (Taylor, 1983):

Stage one
Grouping of children; training children in the use of materials; establishing discipline and control.

Stage two
Using one hour or one block of time to do two specific tasks, the teacher setting the tasks, the children choosing the order and timing.

Stage three
Teacher extending the periods of integration and number of tasks, perhaps doing this one group at a time.

Stage four
Reducing teacher direction, children knowing what tasks to do without being told by the teacher; lengthening the periods of integration; teacher drawing up daily plans for the children.

Stage five

Days of integration moving to a week of integration, perhaps one group at a time; extended use of assignment cards.

One can see that as steps to integration gather momentum so do the management problems, principally that the integrated day is onerous to the teacher (exhausting); can cause high noise levels; requires scrupulous record-keeping by both children and teachers; can let lazy children 'slip through the net'; by having rotating groups, may militate against self-directed work at some stages of moving towards integration; requires very careful planning; requires secure discipline; can cause problems of pupil movement and its concomitant distraction; is often based on assignment cards which can become boring and repetitive, a correspondence course; requires a measure of responsibility and freedom from children which they might not have; might not extract the full potential from the topic or children; needs to ensure some chair-based activities to minimize unnecessary movement.

While the integrated day is predicated on notions of children's autonomy and individualized rates of learning, this should not occlude the planning which the teacher must undertake if it is to be successful. There is clearly an 'invisible pedagogy' (Bernstein, 1977) of secure management at work in the apparent diversity of learning and teaching styles which are embraced by the notion of integration. Perhaps the less overtly structured the situation appears the more structured it has to be covertly. Evaluation will establish how effectively the issues raised in this discussion are being met in the practice and management of the integrated day.

OPEN PLAN ORGANIZATION

The move to integration often matches classroom design where an ideologically more open classroom (Kohl, 1970; Brogden, 1983) is set in a physical layout of open areas, shared spaces and resources, and team management of teaching and learning. Openness extends therefore to management and organizational structures. Flexibility is the key here which unlocks the door to child-centred learning, to empiricist and rationalist epistemologies and to psychological notions of children as active agents of their own learning in a supportive and co-operative social environment. This is well summarized by Bennett, Andreae, Hegarty and Wade (1980), who describe an open plan school as one which facilitates joint use of space and resources and which leads to co-operation between teachers and various groupings of children. Flexibility is revealed in the organization of teaching and learning spaces.

Bennett *et al.* (1980) typified three common arrangements of open plan teaching: 'fully open plan' where divisions of space are made only by low furniture; 'semi open plan' where space is generally open but with teaching areas defined by walls with openings; and 'flexible open plan' where areas can be opened out or closed off by sliding screens. The fluidity of this concept takes itself to pedagogy, where flexible teaching strategies claim the strengths (Brogden, 1983) of: developing pupil autonomy and individuality; maximizing space through shared space; moving away from whole class instruction to activity methods; arranging the environment so that pupils can learn for themselves; facilitating social learning and peer contact; arranging flexible teaching and learning arrangements; facilitating team teaching approaches; enabling team planning; enabling support to be given to less able and inexperienced teachers; saving on resource duplication; providing opportunity for contact between adults; encouraging teacher and pupil co-operation; allowing flexibility of group size; allowing teachers to learn from each other; avoiding feelings of insecurity and isolation which may arise in cellular classrooms, especially with difficult children; allowing children to be taught by more than one teacher; allowing vertical grouping; developing a sense of community; sharing ideas, skills, experiences, successes, problems; harnessing more resources.

It can also bring a train of problems which, unless anticipated and catered for, can frustrate the high ideological appeal of this pedagogic strategy (Hatton, 1985): much transition time; lazy children can go unnoticed; the system might fail if there are weak, unco-operative and uncommitted teachers; children wasting materials; monitoring children's progress is problematic; there could be a lot of noise and distraction; the lack of teacher intervention might cause the full potential of the work to be neglected; the workload on teachers is high; discipline might be difficult; staffing and training might be inadequate; there may be overcrowding; shared space may mean that storage of children's materials and books has to be away from the home base; teachers might not enjoy the necessary visibility in open plan teaching; children may dislike the removal of the security of walls; excessive staff turnover might be more problematic in team situations; cover for absent staff might be problematic; locating quiet rooms might mean children are out of sight of the teacher; the circulation of children might cause congestion; there may be inadequate display space; there may have to be less than one chair for one child; team teaching might impose restrictions on teaching styles; clashes of personality and teaching styles might be more apparent; inexperienced teachers may feel inhibited; time is required for corporate planning; children may take undesirable advantage of the situation; supervision may become a nightmare.

Like the integrated day, then, open plan teaching requires careful plans to be laid for pupils to capitalize on the freedom which theoretically accompanies this type of learning. How the benefits are realized in practice, and how the problem of this form of organization are overcome, form the substance of evaluation.

Criteria for evaluating pedagogy have been set out so far in this chapter. Additionally, the curriculum planner is faced with evaluation questions at an overall level (discussed more fully in Chapter 7) but which can be raised here, to ask the following questions:

1. How are the pedagogical and organizational principles rendered appropriate to the primary ethos?
2. How are the pedagogical and organizational principles rendered appropriate to the aims of the curriculum?
3. How are the pedagogical and organizational principles matched to individual needs, abilities, rates of learning and interests?
4. How clearly are the criteria for evaluating pedagogy defined?
5. What is the balance of consistency, flexibility and variety in the pedagogy?
6. How efficient and effective are the pedagogy and organization for teachers and children?
7. How do the pedagogies and organizations make most efficient use of time, space, and material resources?
8. How are the children likely to be motivated by the pedagogy?
9. How are skills of exposition, questioning, discussion and summary best developed in children and teachers?
10. How do the pedagogy and organization respond to the complexity of task demand?

In conclusion, the primary ethos lends itself in planning pedagogy to a diversity of teaching and learning styles and to different levels and spheres of teacher and child control of learning, supported by a range of organizational and resourcing practices. There is no clear or exclusive relationship between pedagogic styles and epistemologies, ideologies, psychologies or sociologies. Rather it is the interaction of all these elements which renders curriculum planning for primary schools both daunting and exciting. The disarmingly subtle criterion of appropriacy must be applied, the curriculum and pedagogy being appropriate to the task, the learners, the teachers, and the ideological, epistemological, psychological and sociological supports which hold the curriculum in place. The task is to expose and to analyse issues which underlie the concept of matching, which is dealt with in the next chapter.

TIME

Children spend up to thirty-five hours a week at school. It is worth considering how this time might best be used. Time is a critical and finite resource available to the teacher, not to be wasted. In analysing, planning for and evaluating the most valuable use of time, teachers might profitably address the following questions:

1. Is there a timetable?
2. How much flexibility is there in it?
3. Has the day and the week a rhythm and flow?
4. How does the timetable allow for incubation and activities that continue over long periods?
5. How does the timetable cater for individual differences in the class?
6. How much time is there for individual, group and class work?
7. Are there periods of quiet?
8. How does the day begin and end?
9. Should there be a playtime?
10. How are playtimes used?
11. Is time used most effectively?
12. Are the time limits and time scales for the curriculum appropriate and effective?
13. Is time used flexibly to respond to children's learning styles and to different tasks?

SPACE

Many classrooms are too small for the number of children they contain and the variety of activities that takes place. Therefore the way space is used can have a considerable impact on the nature and quality of the learning. In evaluating the planning for the most appropriate use of space, the following questions can be addressed:

1. Is there too much furniture?
2. Is the best use made of the whole space of the school?
3. How does the use of space reflect the range and nature of different activities?
4. How effectively is shared space used?
5. How attractive and stimulating is the space?
6. How does the grouping of tables and work areas reflect the needs of the children and the tasks?
7. How well do children understand the classroom organization?

8. How appropriately and effectively are the resources deployed?
9. How accessible are resources and spaces?
10. How easy is pupil and teacher movement?
11. How effectively does the organization of space promote pupil interaction?

MATERIALS

Materials available should be linked to the areas of experience or curricular areas of the school. Some might be in the classroom while others might be shared. The question of resource allocation, control, location and use must be addressed and evaluated by planners to maximize their benefit. Such evaluation questions could be:

1. How do the resources reflect the range of the curriculum?
2. How do the resources reflect the focus of the curriculum?
3. How do the resources reflect the level of the curriculum for each child?
4. How are the resources organized?
5. How stimulating are the resources?
6. How are they used?
7. How are they maintained?
8. How accessible are they?
9. How appropriate are they to the task?
10. Are they of good quality?
11. Are there sufficient resources?
12. How attractive are the displays?
13. How are displays used for learning?
14. How varied in form and function are the displays?
15. How frequently are displays changed?
16. How is the total classroom used as a learning resource?

CHILDREN

Embodied in the primary ethos is the notion that opportunities should be provided for children to work as a part of the whole class, in groups or individually. The organization of the classroom therefore should encourage the greatest degree of autonomy possible for the children and it is therefore vital that they are familiar with the routines and organizational frameworks, knowing where materials are, how to access them, and the procedures for their return. It is important to develop self-reliance in the children, obviating the need for every decision to be made by and through the teacher. This takes time, certainly, but it is an important educational purpose, as is the recognition on the part of the child that she or he must clear up after an activity.

THE CLASSROOM ETHOS

Everything within the classroom contributes to its ethos − its air of purposefulness, its quality, its variety, its sensitivity. Everything in it or absent from it affects children and their responses. If it is tidy and well organized with a variety of interesting stimuli then this has a positive impact on children's work. If it is sloppy, untidy and lacking in basic organization then this too affects the demeanour of children, unsettling them and demotivating them. The classroom thus should exude a sense of mutual respect and trust.

It is necessary for the teacher to review constantly and critically the environment of the classroom to identify those aspects that might have a detrimental effect on learning, and then to modify them. The whole notion here is of evaluation and self-evaluation, and is dealt with in considerable detail in Chapter 7. At this stage a teacher might consider evaluating:

1. The grouping of furniture, resources and children.
2. Displays.
3. General tidiness.
4. Diversity of arrangements.
5. Relationships and interactions.
6. Learning processes.
7. Learning outcomes.

Children learn as a result of their interaction with their environment, and therefore the environment of the classroom and school, their planned and incidental features, must contribute positively to this process. This accords with the central characteristics of the primary ethos outlined in Chapter 1.

This chapter has outlined the various components over which teachers can exert a substantial measure of control in their curriculum planning. The components are key factors which impinge directly on children, reinforcing the significance of the 'curriculum through the child's eyes' outlined in Chapter 2. The discussion then is moving towards consideration of the impact of the issues raised so far to planning curriculum content and to matching, the subject of the next chapter.

5
MATCHING

In planning the curriculum the notion of matching has to be addressed. At first glance this might appear to be a very specific task carried on by teachers as individuals with their own children. However, this chapter seeks to relate the matching issue to more general levels of curriculum planning, it acts as a bridge between discussions of aims and objectives and detailed curriculum planning at a more highly focused level. Superficially, the concept of matching appears unproblematic, merely matching the task to the child or vice versa. This simplistic notion obscures the many components involved in matching, the many variables which have to be matched with each other at the planning levels and stages. At one level they can be represented as in Figure 5.1.

THE TASK

Initially the type of task has to be clarified before it can be matched to the child. Bennett *et al.* (1984), researching pupils in the seven to nine age range, identified five types of task:

1. Incremental tasks: these 'involve the process of accretion in the acquisition of new facts, skills, rules or procedures' (Bennett *et al.*, 1984, p. 24).
2. Restructuring tasks: here children work mainly with familiar materials but are 'required to discover, invent or construct new ways of looking at a problem' for themselves' (ibid., pp. 24–5).
3. Enrichment tasks: these 'demand the use of familiar knowledge in unfamiliar contexts' (ibid., p. 25), i.e. the application of new knowledge.

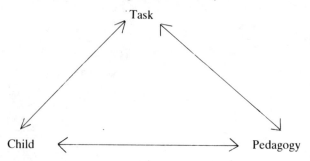

FIGURE 5.1   Components involved in discussing matching

4. Practice tasks: these require 'the repetitive and rapid application of familiar knowledge and skills to familiar settings and problems...to speed up and make automatic processes already in the pupils' repertoire' (ibid., p. 25).
5. Revision tasks: these require bringing back to children's consciousness material and skills learnt some time previously.

If this is taken in conjunction with a second feature of matching − matching the task type to the balance of types of tasks in the curriculum − then significant findings are exposed. Whereas a brisk pace was found in mathematics work, with 1.3 practice tasks for every incremental task, in language work the pace appeared slower, with almost five practice tasks for every incremental tasks. Enrichment tasks only featured in 7 per cent of number tasks and 5 per cent of language tasks, with an almost total absence of restructuring tasks − clearly an imbalance.

Further, in language nearly a quarter of intended incremental tasks were actually practice tasks, with the picture improving for mathematics where only six intended incremental tasks were actually practice tasks. These findings illustrate perhaps poor teacher diagnosis of ability or attainment of children. During the course of a term the researchers found, disturbingly, that the proportion of incremental tasks decreased while practice tasks increased − a tailing off of task demand. Similar results of mismatch are reported by HMI (DES, 1978a, paras. 6.13 to 6.21; 1982b, para. 2.21).

Another way of clarifying the task aspect of the curriculum is offered by HMI (DES, 1985b) who suggest three perspectives on knowledge in the curriculum: areas of knowledge, elements of learning and characteristics of the curriculum. They can be represented diagrammaticaly to clarify their interrelationship in a way which is useful perhaps for curriculum planners (Figure 5.2).

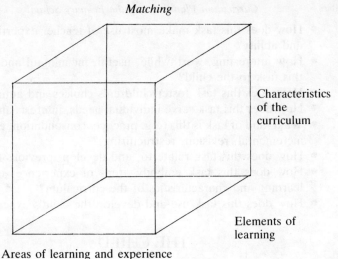

Characteristics
of the
curriculum

Elements of
learning

Areas of learning and experience

FIGURE 5.2 HMI components of the curriculum

Areas of learning and experience comprise: aesthetic and creative; human and social; linguistic and literary; mathematical; moral; physical; scientific; spiritual; technological.

Elements of learning comprise: knowledge; concepts; skills; attitudes.

Characteristics of the curriculum comprise: breadth; balance; relevance; differentiation; progression; continuity; equal opportunities.

Curriculum planners have to keep all three components in mind when building the curriculum, ensuring an appropriate balance and match between the components. Additionally, they have to match the tasks to the contexts and primary ethos established in earlier chapters, to ask the following:

- What are the aims of this task?
- What types of objectives are served by this task?
- How does this task serve instrumental or intrinsic aims?
- What ideologies inform this task?
- Which model of the curriculum does this task emphasize (e.g. content-based, concept-based, skills-based, problem-based, interest-based, objectives-based)?
- How does this task represent an integrated, discipline or subject-bound epistemology?
- How does this task reflect rationalist or empiricist epistemologies?
- How does this task reflect process or product views of knowledge?

- How does this task make most use of teacher expertise, interest and ability?
- How interesting, worthwhile, useful, meaningful and relevant is this task to the child?
- How does this task foster children's choices and autonomy?
- How does this task serve individual needs, interests and abilities?
- What kind of task is this (e.g. practice, consolidation, enrichment, incremental, revision, restructuring)?
- How does this task relate to, and develop, previous tasks?
- How does this task embody areas of experience, elements of learning and characteristics of the curriculum?
- How does this task use and develop the child's experience?

THE CHILD

The types of task, balance of tasks and their relationship to contexts and models of the curriculum have to be matched both to each other and to a further component – the child. In simplistic terms this can be approached in terms of levels of attainment. The Lancaster study (Bennett *et al.*, 1984) focused on three types of attainer: high, medium and low. The results are important. In mathematics only 43 per cent of the work was well matched, with 28 per cent being too difficult and 26 per cent being too easy; in language work only 40 per cent of the work was well matched, with 29 per cent being too difficult and 26 per cent being too easy. Moreover, high attainers were underestimated on 41 per cent of tasks, and low attainers were overestimated on 44 per cent of tasks – figures which cast serious doubt on the extent to which children are allowed to work at their own rates, a central feature of the primary ethos.

Similar findings can be seen in the HMI primary survey (DES, 1978a) and first school survey (DES, 1982b). The picture from the Lancaster study is not improved by the findings that levels of match diminished as children grew older, and that teachers simply did not see that any tasks could be too easy for children, the problem of underestimation was invisible to them (Bennett *et al.*, 1984, p. 49).

Given this alarming degree of mismatch between intention and transaction, there appears to be a cogent need for teachers to review their diagnostic and assessment procedures so that tasks are challenging but not too difficult – the 'moderate novelty' principle mentioned in Chapter 1 – to stretch rather than to dislocate! Matching involves assessment, formal or informal, written or observed; it requires information so that future decisions can be informed by an accurate appraisal of each child.

This raises a fourth element in considering matching, that of assessing and matching performance and potential, and the relationships between them (Alexander, 1984); performance often being measured in narrow terms by tests, and potential being uncertain and difficult to predict.

The need for careful diagnosis and assessment is attested to uncompromisingly by HMI (DES, 1978a, paras. 6.14 to 6.21; 1982b, para. 3.27), where evidence of the best match was found in subjects where the most careful and detailed assessment procedures were in operation − notably well in reading, writing, spoken language, mathematics and music, and poorly in other areas of the curriculum. Such a problematic issue in assessment of performance and potential argues for the need to review the glib definition of matching offered by HMI (DES, 1978a, para. 6.12) as 'the relationship between the standard of work that children in groups were doing and that which they are considered by HMI to be capable of doing in each subject'.

This definition raises more questions than it answers, for it requires an explication of 'relationship', 'standard', 'work', 'doing' and 'capable'. It is unacceptable to take such definitions blandly at face value; each teacher or curriculum planner needs to examine carefully the spectrum of issues involved in the keywords.

A fifth element is introduced into the matching issue when discussing assessment and diagnosis, that of criteria of assessment. What will the teacher assess to determine performance and potential? If the primary ethos of the need to meet individual differences is espoused then an honest assessment must involve a comprehensive analysis of needs, interests and abilities in all senses; indeed, the primary ethos exposes the child potentially to considerably more assessment than a more conservative task or knowledge-centred curriculum, for additionally it requires personality assessment (Sharp, Green and Lewis, 1975).

The issue exposed is the need to match the task not simply to a child's level of attainment or developmental level but to a child's individual needs, interests, abilities and previous experiences, i.e. that which each child brings to the situation, task or activity (Smith, 1975; Harlen, 1980; Morrison, 1984), a central tenet of the primary ethos. This is of course an objective which is laudable in theory but hugely difficult in practice. It requires acute sensitivity to, and knowledge of, the child by the teacher and demands informative record-keeping to ascertain existing knowledge and skills necessary for a teacher to plan the next appropriate course of action for the child.

Nor does the problem rest there, for in raising the need to match children's individual personalities to the tasks, this involves looking at each child's optimum and preferred learning styles (Harlen, 1980) — again a key element of the primary ethos. The ORACLE research (Galton *et al.*, 1980) classified four types of pupil behaviour in classrooms:

'Attention seekers'

'Attention seekers' and their subgroup 'attention getters' represented 19.5 per cent of the total sample. They engage in task-centred activity or routine work for two thirds of the school day, and are characterized by their need for direct teacher contact. Hence such children will leave their seats to queue at the teacher's desk, or wait for the teacher's attention; indeed, their relationships are likely to be more intense with the teacher than with their peers.

'Intermittent workers'

This type made up 35.7 per cent of the sample. These children avoid rather than seek contact with the teacher and have the highest levels of contact with peers than other pupil types. While they spend fairly considerable time on task (64.4 per cent), for 20 per cent of the time they are distracting other children; they appear to lack application.

'Solitary workers'

'Solitary workers' made up 32.5 per cent of the sample. These children interact very frequently with the teacher and their peers but engage in the highest degree of time on task (77.1 per cent). They stay in their base and work quietly, resisting distraction. They are essentially passive, static and co-operative.

'Quiet collaborators'

This type made up 12.3 per cent of the sample. They are characterized by interaction with the teacher not individually but as members of a group, the interactions being task-focused. They interact verbally with their peers relatively infrequently in comparison to intermittent workers, though their time on task is high (72.6 per cent). They rely on teacher support and are prepared to wait for the teacher to give it rather than to work autonomously. They show a tendency to revert to patterns of solitary workers when the teacher is not attending to them directly.

Children may prefer different learning styles, some learning best from a highly structured and logical approach, others from branching, eclectic approaches to learning (c.f. remarks in Chapter 1 about the logical and psychological aspects of learning). Some children's learning may be from a didactic style; for others a problem-solving approach more fairly represents the way they learn; for others an active, experiential style is most suitable. Just as with the 'task' component of matching, the issues in the 'child' component have to be matched to contexts and primary ethos raised in earlier chapters, to ask the following questions:

1. What perspectives of the child and of childhood are being served by the curriculum?
2. How are the principles of the primary ethos being translated into practice for each child?
3. How is the child's motivation being developed and used in this curriculum?
4. How is the child's self-concept being developed and used in this curriculum?
5. How does this curriculum contribute to the development of facets of the child's whole personality?
6. How does this curriculum meet children's individual differences of need, interest, ability and skills?
7. How does this curriculum utilize and develop individual learning styles and rates of learning?
8. How is an enriching social and emotional environment being provided for each child?
9. How is autonomy being developed in the child?
10. How does the organization of the classroom and school foster security in the child? For example, for some children the removal of the security of walls in open-plan classrooms has been likened to the removal of trousers (Bennett *et al.*, 1980)!
11. What models of learning are being developed in each child?

PEDAGOGY

A further factor in the matching issue is raised when considering the level of match or mismatch between learning styles and teaching styles, that of the relationship between pupil types and teaching styles. The effect of teaching styles on learning may be greater than that of pupil styles (Galton *et al.*, 1980). This is important when reflecting that the primary survey (DES, 1978a) found a great emphasis on didactic teaching methods (approximately 75 per cent of teachers mainly used them), while less than 5 per cent relied chiefly on an exploratory approach, and about 20 per cent used a combination of both. A didactic approach could well be totally mismatched to children who learn in a more experiential, eclectic and problem-solving mode. A teaching style is the outcome of a variety of factors, for example:

- Personal attitudes, values and beliefs about children, education, schools, curricula, society;
- Personality;
- Previous experience;
- Resource availability, organization and use;
- Physical layout of the school, e.g. open plan or traditional class-rooms;
- Organization of children, e.g. streamed, mixed ability, vertical grouping;
- Organization of curriculum, e.g. by subjects, integrated days, integration of subject matter, content of the curriculum;
- Management of the school, e.g. leadership, responsibility, motivation, organizational health and climate, school policies and philosophies, teamwork, collegiality, bureaucracy, internal and external environment of the school;
- Political constraints.

A style is reflected on a day-to-day level in:

- Type of activity in the classroom.
- Type of organization of the curriculum.
- Organization of the classroom.
- Level of pupil choice and autonomy.
- Type and use of resources.
- Grouping and organization of children.
- Children's roles in the classroom.
- Nature of teacher involvement with the children.
- Criteria for evaluating and assessing children.
- Nature and amount of pupil and teacher talk.
- Type of teacher behaviour − the strict disciplinarian to the nervous friend.
- Level and type of the discipline.

Hargreaves (1972) distinguishes three types of teacher − liontamers, entertainers and 'new romantics', the characteristics of which can be mapped out on a series of issues which have striking resemblance to the components of ideologies outlined by Meighan (1981) in Chapter 1 (see Figure 5.3). Curriculum planners need to tailor their programmes and proposals to teacher types; teacher types need to tailor their behaviour to curriculum planners. A style evolves in interaction with children; it

Title of style — Component of style	Entertainer	Liontamer	'New romantic'
Content of curriculum	Teacher-controlled integrated topics	Teacher-controlled subjects	Negotiated, individualized, integrated curriculum
Teaching style	Multiple resources, a 'palace of varieties'	Firm discipline, teacher as expert, 'chalk and talk'	Freedom, trust, children naturally motivated, immersion in a topic
Pupil's role	Active, group work, much child-to-child talk	Passive, listening, silent children, children behave uniformly	Children decide their own tasks, intrinsic motivation, children learn to question
Evaluation	Attainment assessed though made as enjoyable as possible	Examinations and marked work, standards, academic achievement	Self-evaluation, feedback and diagnosis
Teacher/pupil relationships	Informal, friendly, open	Formal, cool, distant, conflictual	Equal status and power

FIGURE 5.3   Hargreaves' conception of teaching styles

should be planned to match pupils' learning styles and personalities. How far teaching styles meet pupil needs and optimum learning styles was explored by the ORACLE research (Galton *et al.*, 1980). The researcher found four principle teaching styles:

'Individual monitors'

'Individual monitors' make up 22.4 per cent of the sample. They are characterized by low levels of interaction with groups or the class as a whole; rather they concentrate on individuals, substantially in a didactic vein, telling the children what to do or posing factual rather than open-ended questions. This is a management strategy, as in this style teachers spend much time marking work in the children's presence, which is a constant and pressing need. Relating this to pupil types there is a high proportion (nearly 50 per cent) of 'intermittent workers' in this teaching style, as though the teacher's attention were so taken up with each individual child that she or he could not easily monitor the other children. This is supported in the evidence of the second teaching style, 'class enquirers'.

'Class enquirers'

'Class enquirers' account for 15.5 per cent of the sample. This style of teaching is characterized by class teaching and individualized learning, little interaction with pupils in groups, a high usage of questioning, and a notable incidence of statements related to ideas and problem-solving, all highly controlled and directed by the teacher. In this style the representation of the pupil style 'intermittent workers' is drastically diminished to 9 per cent. This indicated perhaps the teacher's success in reducing the amount of distraction when using this style; the corollary of this is a rise in 'solitary workers' to 65 per cent.

'Group instructors'

'Group instructors' constitute 12.1 per cent of the sample. As its title suggests, it emphasizes teacher instruction with groups — three times more than the other styles; it is distinguished also by a relatively high level of factual statements and verbal feedback. Problem-solving approaches are used, though stress is laid on the informational aspects of the activity. In this teaching style 'attention seekers' are represented the least of all the teaching styles, and 'quiet collaborators' the most of all the teaching styles — a seven to one ratio of 'quiet collaborators' to 'attention seekers'.

'Style changers'

This type make up 50 per cent of the sample. This group is split into three subgroups. 'Infrequent changers' (10.3 per cent of the sample) changed their style only when the occasion demanded, for example, when grouping criteria in the class (e.g. by ability of friendships) failed to be productive or when a particular strategy (e.g. formal didactic teaching) was ready to be changed to a more relaxed style when the children had acquired 'correct' learning habits. This group received the highest order questioning and statements of ideas, and achieved the highest level of interaction of all the styles. This style comes close to an equal representation of all the pupil styles, except 'quiet collaborators' who figure only minimally. It is significant that whereas for 'group instructors' the ratio of seven to one for 'quiet collaborators' to 'attention seekers' respectively is present, for the teaching style 'infrequent changers' almost the exact reverse is true; indeed, 'attention seekers' figure largest here in comparison to all the other styles.

'Rotating changers' (15.5 per cent of the sample) organized children to move round different activities located in different parts of the room at set times during the day. This had the potential to lead to management and discipline problems – significantly in this style there is a high representation of 'intermittent workers'.

The final subgroup of 'style changers' is that of 'habitual changers' (24.2 per cent of the sample). They made regular though often unplanned changes in style, change for change's sake, often in an attempt to reduce undesirable behaviour. This style is also characterized by little questioning or statements of ideas, and has the lowest level of teacher–pupil interaction of all the main styles.

From the research several conclusions were drawn: 'solitary workers' can be best represented in classes taught by 'class enquirers', while 'attention seekers' figure largely in classes taught by 'infrequent changers'; the effect of 'intermittent workers' is largest in classes taught by 'individual monitors' and least in classes taught by 'class enquirers'; 'quiet collaborators' form the largest group in classes taught by 'group instructors'. An overall league table of teaching styles was constructed with reference to tests of basic skills and study skills which presented the most successful teaching styles (Figure 5.4).

The significance of the ORACLE survey is to point to the need to match the teaching and the learning style, the task to the pedagogy (DES, 1982b). Here one has to question how far 'individual monitors' fairly embody the primary ethos, or whether children's individual differences might be best served by other teaching styles. There is a need for clear criteria to be established in grouping children so that optimum match is obtained between the task, the child and the pedagogy, in order for the child to extract most benefit from the situation. These criteria could include age, ability, friendship, stage of work, focus of tasks, interest in the task, and willingness to work in a group (Kerry and Sands, 1982).

	Position in basic skills test	Position in study skills tests
Infrequent changers	1=	4
Class enquirers	1=	2
Group instructors	3	5
Individual monitors	4	3
Habitual changers	5=	1
Rotating changers	5=	6

FIGURE 5.4 Success in teaching styles measured by performance in basic skill tests by children

This will involve the teacher in planning the sizes of the groups, their composition, their monitoring, and a consideration of the teacher's own role in group work, for example, organizing, directing, controlling, questioning, clarifying, summarizing, stimulating and prompting (see Chapter 4).

There is a need also to ensure appropriate matching between preparation offered at initial training level and subsequent teaching placements in schools – a need endorsed by HMI (DES, 1982c). Moreover, improvements of match and pedagogy require meeting teachers' needs, personalities, backgrounds and preferred modes of operating as well as those of the children, sensitizing both parties to each other. This comes through careful school placement and a reflexive attitude by staff.

The notion of match in pedagogy has to extend to cover issues raised in earlier chapters. Pedagogy embodies the primary ethos and ideological, epistemological, psychological, sociological and managerial contexts, concerns and models of curriculum planning. Curriculum planners attempting to match pedagogy to these may need to ask the following questions:

1. How does this teaching and learning style reflect a concern with content and process?
2. How does this teaching and learning style reflect planning which is skills-based, concepts-based, content-based, problem-based, interest-based, objectives-based?
3. What is the ideological commitment of this teaching and learning style in its view of aims, content, pedagogy, teacher's and pupil's roles, use of resources and organization of children?
4. What is the epistemological commitment of this teaching and learning style in its views of empiricism and process, learning by experience, its attention to enquiry and discovery methods, its development of 'knowing that' and 'knowing how'?
5. In what ways and in what areas of the curriculum are children learning by practical activity?
6. How are the problem-solving and investigational approaches being adopted in the pedagogy?
7. How is an enriching social environment being developed in the curriculum?
8. How do these teaching and learning styles derive from the philosophy, policy and aims of the school?
9. How do these teaching and learning styles make effective use of time, space and organization of the school?
10. How much effective use is being made of staff with particular skills, expertise and abilities?

11. How far are children's optimum learning styles being catered for in this curriculum?
12. How far are teachers' teaching styles being catered for in this curriculum?
13. How flexible are the teaching arrangements, e.g. team teaching, specialist teaching?
14. What resources are being used by teachers and children, e.g. materials, time, space, staff, environment?
15. How are resources being used by teachers and children?
16. How much control over their learning do the children have?
17. How far is the teaching and learning interesting and challenging?

CONCLUSION

The purpose in matching, then, is to bring as close together as possible in the primary school intention and actuality, aims and practice, rhetoric and reality. The model presented at the start of the chapter (Figure 5.1) can be augmented (Figure 5.5). Underlying this model is the continual need for diagnosis, observation, assessment, monitoring and critical awareness of classroom transactions. The curriculum planner seeking to establish an appropriate match in the activities for children is faced, then,

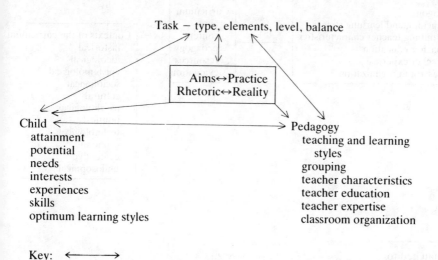

FIGURE 5.5 Expanded version of components involved in discussing matching

with a deeper set of issues than perhaps initially envisaged. It requires attention both to macro and micro influences on the curriculum, in short a 'situational analysis' (Skilbeck and Harris, 1976), which affects the detailed curriculum planning for each class or child – the substance of Chapter 6.

Hence a more fully worked out model of the components in the matching debate, which adds to the level one model at the beginning of the chapter, can be represented as in Figure 5.6. Thus in addressing the

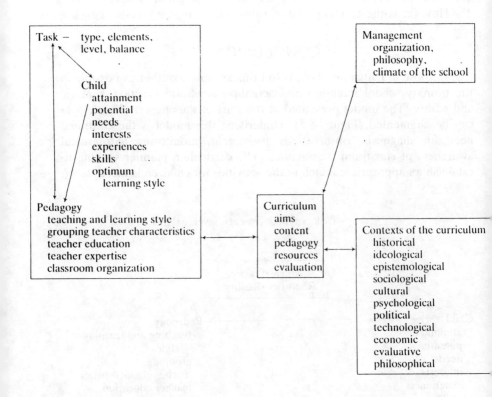

Key: ←——————→
        matched to

FIGURE 5.6 Worked out analysis of components involved in discussing matching

concept of 'match' in curriculum planning an all-embracing version must be adopted; this preserves the central concerns of this book, that the curriculum must be negotiable and that teachers and planners must be open to critical and thoughtful debate.

6
PLANNING CURRICULUM CONTENT

The model presented at the end of Chapter 1 saw the transacted curriculum as the outcome of macro and micro factors bearing on several curricular dimensions. In taking the discussion to issues of curriculum content, several critical questions are raised. Given that not everything can or should go into the curriculum, planners will have to be selective and to justify their selection. The issues here have been aired in Chapter 1: whether one wishes to serve society, preserve traditional and perhaps arcane knowledge, to anticipate future society and cultures, or to concentrate on child-centredness. Attempts have been made to serve all interests (Lawton, 1983; DES, 1985b; Hewlett, 1986; Lawton 1986), though they are not all without criticism.

The value of Lawton's 'cultural analysis' model has been questioned (Whitty, 1985) on four counts: first, for glossing over the role and importance of conflict in society in preference to a curriculum statement which is bland and which seeks a consensus which may be counterproductive; second, for providing an inadequate analysis of issues and conceptions of class; third, for an inadequate analysis of the relationship between education and equality in society; finally, for failing to offer suggestions which will break down inequality in society through education.

Similarly, the HMI 'areas of experience' have attracted criticism (University of Leeds, 1985; Hewlett, 1986; Morrison, 1987) on six counts: initially for reinforcing traditional curricula, schooling and curriculum debate; second, for striving for consensus at the expense of the value of conflict and difference; third, for accepting DES centralism as a *fait accompli*; fourth, for being unclear on its philosophical and sociological origins and justifications; fifth, for elevating the importance of technology too highly; finally, for operating at a level of generality which offers little real assistance to curriculum planners.

The impact and implications of these criticisms can be addressed by curriculum planners on three levels. Initially they may point to the need for a radical redrafting of the curriculum. Such a proposition has been addressed by Hewlett (1986) who discusses 'regions of application' to replace 'areas of experience', focusing on the social utility of children's knowledge: the domestic sphere; the world of work; leisure; continuing education research and exploration; neighbourhood and community education; education about the wider social world – social, political, economic and physical; education about the family; personal relationships in formal and informal spheres; self/personal relationships, the spiritual dimension.

Second, they point to the need to regard any prescriptions as tentative, incomplete and in need of further refinement and extension. Third, this reflects a major theme of this book, that curriculum planning is an ongoing debate rather than a production of a final and unchangeable plan; it is negotiable and subject to scrutiny. Hence the discussion on issues involved in planning curriculum content which follows should serve that notion of a curriculum plan as a proposal. In looking at issues in deciding curriculum content there are many process factors which have to be considered.

COMMONALITY AND INDIVIDUALISM

The same set of constraints and contexts in the curriculumn debate can give rise to diverse practices; indeed, such variety is the embodiment of the primary ethos at individual teacher and child levels. The question then is raised for curriculum planners of whether, in the face of such potential variety, a measure of commonality in decision-making about curriculum content across schools, teachers and pupils can and ought to exist. If it can exist then at what level ought it to operate: commonality of aims, concepts, skills, pedagogy, attitudes, areas of knowledge, or organizations of knowledge? Therefore, in planning curriculum content the balances between consistency, commonality and individualism have to be struck.

At the level of knowledge planners will have to ask, for example, how acceptable it is for a child in school A to study a topic on 'railways' while a child in school B does not, or whether a ten-year-old one year will study something different from a ten-year-old in the following year. The debate is ideological – how far child-centredness can tolerate such differences and whether in the long run teachers do children a service by allowing such flexibility.

Educational aims such as those expressed in Chapter 3 can endure over the years, while knowledge, practices, skills and pedagogy may change. At an epistemological level, too, only limited solace can be found for curriculum planners anxious to secure an identifiable delineation of content from the classifications of knowledge set out in Chapter 2, for while they are marked by similarity of title this can conceal a wide variety of expressions in practice both within and between titles. For example, the aesthetic and creative areas of the curriculum could be totally different in two schools or two classrooms; the 'back to basics' conservatism of one teacher could support mathematical practices which are anathema to a more open-ended, progressivist ideology of another mathematics teacher; one teacher's topic on 'ourselves' may be completely different from another's; the language curriculum of one class may appear on a formal timetable where in another class it does not appear *per se* but has permeated the curriculum.

The management question for the school is to decide on the degree and level of commonality or variety of the curriculum content. In practice there may be a high level of consensus at the levels of aims and definitions of the areas of learning (Ashton *et al.*, 1975; Wicksteed and Hill, 1979), but such consesus ought not perhaps to be left to fortune. Curriculum planners have to resolve questions of individual teachers' freedoms, collegially taken decisions, curriculum responsibility posts and power structures which may coexist in tension rather than consensus.

In some areas of the school there may well be curriculum commonality which is determined by resources – e.g. the mathematics or reading schemes for the whole school, specialist teachers for music or PE, materials for art, craft and design, computing facilities. In other areas the problem at the level of knowledge is less tractable, for the art of teaching and the primary ethos supports the value of individual teachers being free to decide and interpret curricular guidelines. This is problematic, for the inclusion and exclusion of knowledge has to be justified. The realm of 'topic work' is notoriously difficult here, for without whole school planning it could become fragmented, superficial and repetitive over the primary years (Blyth *et al.*, 1976; DES, 1978a, 1982b).

However, even if one does produce curricula on content terms to avoid this (e.g. Figure 6.1), one still cannot guarantee that the problems of teacher interpretation and choice destroying commonality will be overcome. One teacher's work on 'castles' (year two) may be totally a book study, while another teacher's may be largely observational and practical. Simi-

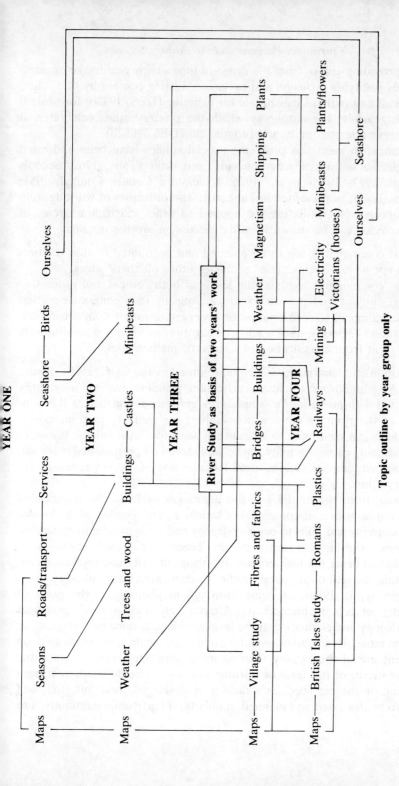

FIGURE 6.1 Curriculum devised in content terms for a junior department

larly, providing choice from the range of topics each year in the example involves justifying inclusion and exclusion. Listing content by title, then, is difficult and perhaps inadequate for planning (DES, 1982b) for while it accords teachers the autonomy which the primary ethos celebrates, it risks neglecting continuity and progression (DES, 1982b).

Attempts to meet this problem in social studies have been addressed through the notion of 'key concepts' and skills (Taba, 1962; Schools Council, 1973; Blyth *et al.*, 1976; Lancashire County Council, 1981; Waters, 1982), as presented in Table 6.1. The principles of working from key concepts and skills can be applied to other curriculum areas, of course. What can be drawn from the discussion are the notions:

1. That commonality has to be planned and negotiated so that teachers are not merely recipients or agents of other planners' ideas.
2. That commonality exists at the levels of both content and process.
3. That content and process exist symbiotically in a context, e.g. that observation in science is *scientific* observation rather than artistic observation (Jenkins, 1987), and classification in history is qualitatively different from classification in science or mathematics.

The notion of commonality is well represented by the CDC (1980) (Figure 6.2). At a philosophical level curriculum planners are not necessarily presented with an 'either/or' situation − *either* commonality *or* the principles of the primary ethos which support individuality and autonomy. Individuals can contribute to collective collegial decision-making; discovery methods and practical activity can be well served on pre-planned curricula. Commonality implies sharing at all levels − one of the key tenets of the primary ethos.

Missing from the model and the discussion so far is the question of whether the notion of commonality should extend beyond aims, knowledge, concepts and skills to cover pedagogy and evaluation − its principles, purposes, criteria, foci and methods. Teachers may well see such an extension as being the final erosion into their authority and professionality, as setting the seal of approval on the 'teacher-proof' curriculum so questionable in the 1970s, as being thorough in planning to the point of pedantry, or as being unnecessary. Alternatively, a measure of agreement on pedagogy and evaluation at the level of principle must be unavoidable. For example, if an environmental studies curriculum is predicated on frequent use of the locality − using more than one teacher − then the relative merits of this form of learning will have to be debated; or if team teaching or subject specialist teaching is envisaged then this, too, will need to be discussed and planned. Similarly, if curriculum continuity is to

TABLE 6.1 Key concepts and skills for topic work

Taba (1962)	**Schools Council (1973)**	**Blyth et al. (1976)**
Causality	Developing interests,	Communication
Conflict	attitudes and	Power
Co-operation	aesthetic awareness	Values and beliefs
Cultural change	Observing, exploring,	Conflict/consensus
Difference	and ordering	Similarity/differences
Interdependence	observations	Continuity/change
Modification	Developing basic	Cause and consequence
Power	concepts and logical	
Societal control	thinking	
Traditions	Posing questions and	
Values	devising experiments	
	or investigations to	
	answer them	
	Acquiring knowledge	
	and skills	
	Communicating	
	Appreciating patterns	
	and relationships	
	Interpreting findings	
	critically	

Lancashire County Council (1981)
1. Learning about living things:
   plants, seeds, trees, mosses, fungi, seaweeds, animals, insects, fish, birds
2. Learning about ourselves:
   body, food, looking after ourselves (health), social behaviour, reproduction
3. Learning about the immediate environment:
   buildings, transport, services, pollution
4. Learning about the weather and seasons
5. Learning about energy:
   sound, magnetism, electricity, water, heat, air, light, mechanics,
      conservation of energy
6. Learning about the properties of materials:
   structure, appearance, strength, change, flexibility, effect of water,
   magnetism, effect of light, effect of sound, electrical conductance, heat
   conductance

Waters (1982)
Investigative skills
Study skills
Manipulative skills
Creative skills
Communication skills
Personal and social development

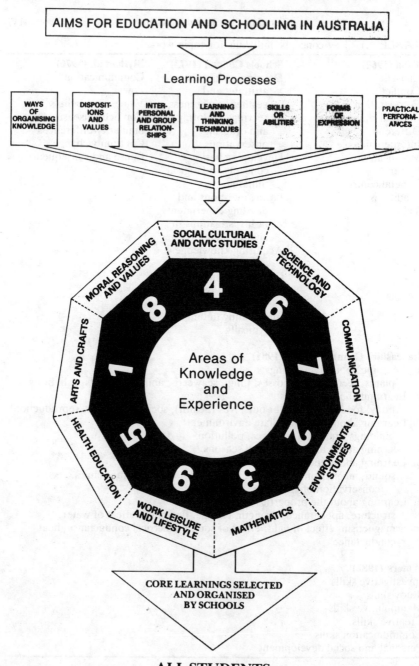

(Source: CDC (1980) *Core Curriculum for Australian Schools*, Canberra, p. 20)

FIGURE 6.2 A core curriculum for Australian schools

be taken beyond the level of summary epithets and thumbnail sketches then evaluation will have to be planned and agreed.

INTEGRATION AND FRAGMENTATION

Curriculum planners have to decide on the extent of, and relationship between, an integrated and a subject-separate curriculum, The primary ethos has been seen to support an integrated curriculum for various reasons:

1. It accords with the way in which children view the world (Waters, 1982).
2. Children unify rather than atomize knowledge in their minds by assimilating new knowledge to existing knowledge (Wheeler, 1967).
3. The 'whole personality' is best served by a holistic approach to the curriculum.
4. It opens up channels of investigation which subject specialist curriculum boundaries may close.
5. It facilitates a rhythm of learning so that individual rates and types of learning are not strangled by constantly switching subjects (Pring, 1976).
6. Knowledge is unfairly represented as discrete packages – relationships are implicit between areas and dimensions of knowledge (CACE, 1967).
7. Children are given power to decide and pursue their own learning paths (Schools Council, 1972).
8. It facilitates the study of complex human issues (ibid.).
9. Key concepts can straddle subject boundaries (Taba, 1962; CACE, 1967).

On the other hand, the notion of integration as complementing the 'natural and given' development of the child has been challenged at a philosophical level by Walkerdine (1983) who argues that 'we must view as a production, rather than as an uncovering, those characteristics which define the normal and natural individual' (p. 85) – that 'natural' qualities are in fact social constructions. Similarly, Alexander (1984) suggests that 'the environment is "integrated" only if we choose to view it that way' (p. 70). Integration is as much a construct as subject separation. On an ideological or sociological level, integration has been opposed by a conservatism anxious to retain the traditional curriculum and the greater power which traditional subject teaching accorded teachers (Bernstein, 1971). On an ideological and epistemological level it has been argued (Morrison, 1986a) that subject specialism may in fact serve a child's individual needs and interests more than a generalized and integrated curriculum. On a psychological and epistemological level, Entwistle (1970) suggests that 'integrated studies seem a poor instrument for acquiring knowledge and skill in a manageable, disciplined form' (p. 110). Indeed, Whitehead (1932) offers 'generalization' as the stage of learning which follows rather then precedes the precision of subject teaching.

Eggleston and Kerry (1985) echo this in their comment that 'if pupils are engaged in some integrated or interdisciplinary study it is difficult to see how they could make sense of experiences or knowledge without benefit of the conceptual structures which disciplines provide' (p. 83).

On a political level, subject specialist teaching is being advocated for children in their later primary years (DES, 1978a, 1983, 1985c) as an attempt to bring depth of study into the curriculum. Curriculum planning and decision-making will have to resolve the relationship between subject teaching and integrated curricula: whether they can complement each other rather than being alternatives (Entwistle, 1970) or whether the two are in a relationship of tension (Morrison, 1985). The primary ethos supports teacher and child autonomy, individual needs, interests, expertise and intrinsic motivation. This may best be realized through subject-centred teaching (Morrison 1986a) as well as through an integrated curriculum. While subject teaching may embody the principles of the disciplined enquiry outlined in Chapter 1, it should not be allowed to sacrifice the principles of the primary ethos − flexibility, originality, diversity − to uniformity and outworn subject matter (ibid.). If subject teaching is to operate (which may well be the case) then clear links between subjects will have to be drawn where possible, requiring teachers to discuss, negotiate and plan corporately (Morrison, 1985), key elements of a healthy school climate (see Chapter 1).

Content and process can come together in subject teaching through the notion of guided discovery, for in the hands of specialist teachers such learning can be more exciting for children than an integrated curriculum taught by generalists. The limitations of this approach start where child-centredness is equated with a child-chosen curriculum, for children may select work which does not fall comfortably into a specialist's domain. Here perhaps the notion of generalist teachers with specific expertise which can be tapped by both pupils and teachers is useful − a far more open utilization of staff than in many traditional classrooms. Curriculum planners will have to decide how to implement such principles to best advantage.

Constructing a Matrix

One way of planning within a subject is by contructing a matrix. In art education, for example, a matrix to ensure comprehensive coverage at the planning stage could be presented as in Figure 6.3 (DES, 1983b). In matrix planning for subjects it may be useful to list the content in the columns and the intellectual and affective skills in the rows (c.f. earlier discussion of Bloom's taxonomy in Chapter 3). For example in science one can construct a matrix from Table 6.1 and present it for planning purposes as in Figure 6.4.

If an integrated curriculum is being planned then the 'integrative threads' (Taba, 1962) for that curriculum have to be decided. What is the common focus through which various curriculum elements are brought together? There are a variety of 'threads' available: key concepts can be set and defined and returned to at ever increasing levels of complexity and abstraction in a 'spiral curriculum' (Bruner, 1960) (see Figure 6.5).

Second, there is the integration of learning and experience provided by resources, e.g. the home corner, the painting area, the library. Third, integration can be reached through the notion of an activity or group of activities, e.g. growing plants in different environments, visiting a farm, where a range of skills and forms of representation (c.f. Bruner in Chapter 1) are brought to focus on the activity (Figure 6.6).

Fourth, a problem-centred approach (Waters, 1982) can be an integrating principle (c.f. Chapter 2 on problem-based planning) where children learn to 'approach social problems from a number of different angles and to see experience from as many relevant facets as possible, so that they resist prejudiced conclusions or simple solutions' (Entwistle, 1970, p. 110).

Fifth, on a smaller scale, centres of interest can be used to integrate experiences, where for example by careful questioning, discussion, display and addition of children's work, a collection of shells or leaves can provide a stimulating environment for children − one of the features of the primary ethos developed in Chapter 5.

Sixth, the notion of integration can extend to cross-curricular planning, e.g. language or mathematics across the curriculum (DES, 1974, 1982b). Curriculum planners can approach this conceptually through matrix planning (Figure 6.7), where, for example, mathematics across the areas of

	Creating, making	Appreciating, evaluating	Practising	Introducing, knowledge of	Synthesizing	Co-operating
Experience of terms colour line shape texture form tone spatial relations						
Experience of media oil water chalk crayon clay plaster wood fabric paper card thread linoleum Plasticene wire metal plastic						
Manipulative skills cutting glueing sewing knitting weaving printing dyeing painting drawing shaping enamelling firing glazing						

FIGURE 6.3   Matrix planning for an art curriculum

experience can be ascertained by reading across the mathematics row, or where for instance the relationship of the 'aesthetic and creative' area to the other areas can be planned. This can be taken further, where each area is broken down into its constituent parts. For example, in language work a matrix could be set out as in Table 6.2. The principle can be applied to other areas of the curriculum.

	Developing interests, attitudes and aesthetic awareness	Observing, exploring, ordering observations	Developing basic concepts and logical thinking	Posing questions and devising experiments or investigations to answer them	Acquiring knowledge and skills	Communicating	Appreciating patterns and relationships	Interpreting findings critically
Living things								
Ourselves								
Immediate environment								
Weather and seasons								
Energy								
Properties of materials								

FIGURE 6.4 Matrix planning in a science curriculum

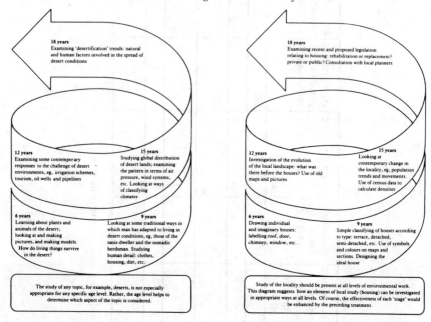

(Source: Inner London Education Authority (1981) *The Study of Places in the Primary School*, p. 4.)

FIGURE 6.5   A spiral curriculum approach to curriculum planning

There are further 'essential issues' which DES (1985b) suggest should cross the curriculum even though they pay relatively scant attention to them throughout the document (Morrison, 1987). These then can become the basis for matrix planning (Table 6.3). The principle of establishing cross-curricular links or issues which permeate the curriculum is vital at the planning stage otherwise it risks being lost or neglected in the practical implementation of the curriculum.

Seventh, integration can be achieved through the multidisciplinary 'topic' or 'project' (e.g. trees, the locality, ourselves) where the topic draws on several areas of the curriculum (see Figure 6.8). Here the planning draws comprehensively on the discussion in Chapter 2 on tactical levels of planning, for additional to the 'areas of experience' upon which the topic draws should be statements of levels and types of thinking (c.f. Bloom's taxonomies discussed in Chapter 3): aims and objectives, skills, concepts, activities, attitudes, social and personal development, sequences

The activity-based project

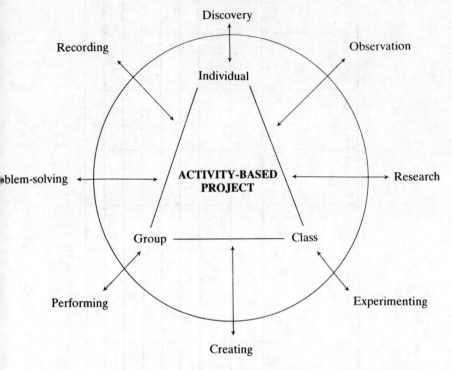

(Source: Waters, 1982, *Primary School Projects: Planning and Development* p. 21.)

FIGURE 6.6 Activity-based curriculum planning

of learning – all components of the matching debate. Thus the notion of a topic is an organizational strategy.

Curriculum planners will have to decide where an integrated approach fits most comfortably, for to try to integrate artificially or to press all areas of the curriculum unthinkingly or at whatever cost into the service of spurious integration is a recipe for a poor curriculum at both theoretical and practical levels. Integration must be appropriate to the aims, curriculum content and components in the matching debate rather than contrived. In decision-making about the organization and structure of the curriculum content, then, planners are driven again to weigh theoretical, epistemological, ideological and practical issues. On a management level curriculum planners will need to decide how resources of time, staff, money, space

	Aesthetic and creative	Human and social	Linguistic and literary	Mathematical	Moral	Physical	Scientific	Spiritual	Technological
Aesthetic and creative									
Human and social									
Linguistic and literary									
Mathematical									
Moral									
Physical									
Scientific									
Spiritual									
Technological									

FIGURE 6.7 Matrix planning from HMI areas of experience

TABLE 6.2 Areas of a language curriculum which could be put into matrix form across the HMI areas of experience (DES, 1985a)

Reading
Reading to gain an overall impression of a single passage or chapter
Reading to select information relevant to a particular topic
Reading to expand on information previously supplied
Reading to follow a sequence of instuctions
Reading to identify answers to questions by direct reference to a given text
Reading to detect information implied in a given passage
Reading to interpret and evaluate a writer's assumptions, intentions, to show
    awareness of characteristics of different kinds of writing
Reading for pleasure
Reading different types of literature

Writing

Describing	Explaining
Narrating	Expounding
Recording	Planning
Reporting	Eliciting
Persuading	
writing for various audiences	
writing in various forms	

Speaking

Questioning	Describing	Clarifying
Expressing	Instructing	Dramatically presenting
Directing	Informing	Discussing
Expounding	Narrating	Explaining
Arguing	Presenting	
Conversing	Recalling	

Listening
Carrying out instructions
Comprehending ideas and expanding on them
Participating in discussions ('active listening')
Maintaining listening span
Following plot and line of argument
Listening responsively to a story and to poetry

and materials are to be best deployed if an integrated or separated curriculum is to operate.

CHARACTERISTICS OF THE CURRICULUM

The planning of the content of the primary curriculum will need to bear certain hallmarks or characteristics. While many of these have been addressed already, there are several other current 'catchwords' which can

TABLE 6.3   HMI essential issues which permeate the areas of experience

Environmental education

Health education

Information technology

Political education

Education in economic understanding

Preparation for the world of work

Careers education

Equal opportunities

Education of ethnic minority children

---

be used as referents in the curriculum debate, notably provided by HMI (DES, 1985b): breadth, balance, relevance, differentiation, progression and continuity.

Breadth

While much of this discussion has been rehearsed in the section on commonality and individualism, there are additional issues which can be raised. DES (1985b) suggest that breadth should obtain across and within all areas of experience, elements of learning and essential issues in the curriculum. The problem of interpretation of these terms has already been met, asking what mathematics, what art and design, what history, etc. Additionally, breadth can be extended to cover pedagogic styles, classroom organization, learning processes, assessment techniques, aims and objectives, ideologies and epistemologies.

Given such a wide field of application of the term, curriculum planners are driven again to decide the dimensions in which breadth of curriculum operates; to consider the selection of content which they make for the curriculum; and to decide on minimum levels of content and dimensions beyond which breadth is lost.

The concept of breadth suggests both a broadening of the notion of 'basic skills' to incorporate more than the 'three Rs' and the view that the 'three Rs' can be taught through a wide curriculum (DES, 1978a). Planners will have to decide whether breadth of the curriculum is best achieved through subject teaching or by integration, through specialist or generalist teachers.

ideas: Wheels   − how they work, axles
                     − their use in machines
                     − wheels as one of a set of circular objects
    Events, visits − one or two of the following:
                  Garage/seeing wheel change
                  Farm or farming museum
                  Railway station or railway museum
                   − a display of wheels would be set up

GUISTIC AND LITERACY
es − some taped for individual
tening
elopment of vocabulary
ing − bus ticket

HUMAN AND SOCIAL
Wheels used to help us − transport,
simple machines
Wheels in old vehicles (farm carts,
etc.)
Working with wheels (potter,
miller)

WHEELS

THEMATICS
e − circles, pattern work
table − bus play
ey
s of sequence − steps in
anging a wheel
ber of wheels on a vehicle

AESTHETIC AND CREATIVE
Representations of wheeled
vehicles in two and three
dimensions
Pattern making/printing − circles
Poems
Songs, action songs, listening to
sounds

RAL
peration in play − bus play
d safety − devising rules

TECHNOLOGY
Layouts for vehicles (cars/trains)
Route for wheeled toy traffic −
outdoor
Construction work (various
challenges to make wheeled
toys, etc.)
Examine simple machines − egg
whisk, hand drill, wheels on
tricycle

SICAL
ugh all art/craft work, making
d modelling activities
ity to steer, turn a vehicle
with hoops
e scale construction − bus, train

SCIENCE
Wheels − simple inclined plane or
chute
Energy − power that causes toy
cars to move − push, friction,
clockwork, twisted elastic,
battery
Cooking − use of whisk

RITUAL
of natural forces − wind/windmill,
ter/waterwheel

FIGURE 6.8   A topic web for a nursery class

Apart from the notion that breadth should not be sacrificed to depth, there is an added difficulty in the term 'breadth', as there is with many of the terms here from HMI, for it may lie uncomfortably with the notions of individual needs, differences and interests encapsulated in the primary ethos. The question arises of whether a child's individuality may be better served by a broad or a narrow curriculum. Hence the notion of breadth may be disjunctive with 'relevance' or 'differentiation'; the issues may exist in tension rather than harmony.

In evaluating breadth in the curriculum, planners can address the following questions; these are arranged for convenience into management and curricular issues.

Management issues

1. Who will take the decisions on breadth?
2. How will breadth be planned, managed, implemented, realized, monitored, recorded and evaluated?
3. What preparations are necessary before staff can discuss breadth? How can the climate for such discussions be set?
4. How will breadth be ensured across the year/school/schools?
5. How will subject teaching and subject specialist teaching be managed to ensure breadth?
6. In whose terms will breadth be discussed and decided?

Curriculum issues

1. How far is breadth a desirable aim of the curriculum?
2. In what terms will breadth be discussed (e.g. epistemological, ideological, cultural, pedagogical, knowledge, concepts, skills, attitudes, areas of experience, regions of application, subjects)?
3. How will the constituents of breadth be decided and prioritized?
4. How will consistency of breadth be ensured?
5. What is the relationship of breadth and depth?
6. How will breadth be ensured in the child's mind?
7. What is the relationship of breadth and differentiation for individual needs and interests, generalism and specialism?

Balance

While the curriculum is to be broad it is also to be balanced. Initially, this entails a realization that balancing a curriculum does not necessarily entail giving equal amounts, both in quantity and time, for each area of experience, element of learning or essential issues. Just as a balanced diet involves eating different amounts of different types of food, the analogy can be extended to the curriculum and its components (Kelly, 1986). Who will decide on the ingredients of the curriculum cake? The further difficulty for the curriculum is to decide the constituents and the relative amounts of curriculum components.

To compound the difficulty the primary ethos, with its notions of individual needs and differences, suggests that children and teachers all have different dietary needs and interests (Kelly 1986, p. 149–50). One child's balance is another child's imbalance; balance and commonality do not always go together. The problem is not solely theoretical. The teacher is constantly faced with the ideological problem of how much latitude to give to children's choice, e.g. in a reception class why should the teacher intervene to move a child on from one type of learning experience to another — the wet area to the jigsaw puzzles — when the child is not interested in jigsaws at that time? How can teachers be certain that a child is covering the range of the curriculum areas of experience when that child follows activities in ways not fully envisaged by the teacher?

The problem here is that of ensuring that the curriculum as planned becomes the curriculum as practised by the children. Balance must exist in the child's mind as well as with the teacher. Thus either balance needs to be tempered by individualization or perhaps balance in the curriculum needs to be seen as only achievable through seeking the lowest common denominator of curriculum components. If this latter is the case then the concept of balance may lead to a bland, undifferentiated and perhaps irrelevant curriculum. Again this reinforces a tension between balance and relevance and differentiation. There has to be a balance between need and content area. The constituents of the 'appropriate' balance for each child are problematic.

HMI (DES, 1985b) provides little assistance in resolving this problem, for its recommendations that balance is achieved through 'appropriate attention to, and sufficient time on, each area, or through each area being "fully developed"' (para. 112) offer little to guide planners anxious to ascertain what 'appropriate attention' or 'sufficient time' is or what it is to be 'fully developed'. In one sense — fortuitously perhaps — HMI is suggesting that these terms have to be negotiated and debated, one of the main features of primary curriculum planning.

In deciding what has to be balanced one cannot remain solely with the terms provided by HMI — areas of experience, elements of learning and characteristics of the curriculum; there are additional factors. The discussion throughout the book has suggested that balances must be struck between ideologies – individual and societal needs – epistemologies (rationalism and empiricism), process and content, breadth and depth, theory and practice (Kelly, 1986), types and levels of skills, subject-bound and integrated curricula, specialism and generalism, the curriculum as derived from forms of knowledge (Hirst, 1965) and cultural analysis (Lawton, 1983), working class and middle class curricula, representations of subcultures, cognitive and affective demands, commonality and individuality, pedagogic styles, organizational practices, autocratic and collegial planning.

This takes the curriculum planner back to reviewing the whole concept of 'match' in Chapter 5. It raises too the question of how far the demand for balance is a demand for compromise – ideological, epistemological, cultural, managerial, curricular – and how far such compromise is necessary or desirable. The notion of balance is integrative; it runs through the discussion of the other characteristics of the curriculum.

In evaluating balance in the curriculum, planners could address the following questions, again for convenience arranged by management and curriculum issues.

Management issues

1. How will balance be ensured across the year/school/schools?
2. How will the ground be laid to discuss balance among staff?
3. How will balance be planned, managed, implemented, realized, monitored, recorded and evaluated?
4. Who will decide on the terms and nature of the balance(s)?
5. In whose terms will the concept of balance be discussed and decided?

Curriculum issues

1. How far is balance a desirable aim of the curriculum?
2. How will the balance be struck between integrated and subject-bound knowledge?
3. What are the terms for discussing balance (e.g. knowledge, concepts, skills, attitudes, elements of learning, areas of experience, regions of application, disciplines, experiences, ideologies, epistemologies, pedagogies, organizations)?
4. In what terms will the balance(s) be struck between relevance, differentiation, individual needs and interests and abilities, received and reflexive curricula, types of task (incremental, practice, revision, application, enrichment, problem-solving, investigational), teacher decision and pupil choice?
5. In what terms will the balance be struck between innovation and existing practice (e.g. ideologies, ideas, epistemologies, curriculum

structures, organizations, managements, pedagogies, continuity and discontinuity, content and process, processes and outcomes, breadth and depth)?
6. How will planners ensure that balance avoids resulting in low-level confusion of practices and epistemologies?

Relevance

The concept of relevance accords with the notion of matching, as the answer to the questions 'relevant to what?' and 'relevant to whom?' will demonstrate. While HMI (DES, 1985b) veils its discussion in generalities (e.g. 'relevant in the sense that it is seen by pupils to meet their present and prospective needs' (para. 116)), curriculum planners require more than this. One can suggest that curriculum content ought to be relevant to:

- Individual and social needs (not necessarily discrete areas).
- School ethos, aims, organization, staff education and vocationalism.
- Ideologies and epistemologies.
- Building motivation and self-concept in children.

The primary ethos, underscoring the notion of relevance, suggests the need to meet individual needs and abilities. However, this raises the problem that what constitutes relevance for one child could well be totally irrelevant to another's needs, interests or abilities. Who is to be the arbiter in such a problem – the child, the teacher, the planner? Will the decision be taken for the child? Will the ideology of the child-chosen curriculum have to be replaced with a curriculum planned in their interests (Peters, 1967)? Do teachers allow the child the choice of not to follow a curriculum, to move out of the frame of reference? Further, how will the problem be resolved if the planner sees that providing a relevant curriculum for each child means providing an unbalanced or narrow curriculum? As with other notions the concept of relevance is seen to run uneasily with differentiation; the HMI terms may coexist in tension.

In evaluating the notion of relevance in the curriculum, planners can address the following questions, arranged in management and curriculum issues.

Management issues
1. How will relevance be ensured across the year/school/schools?
2. How will relevance be planned, managed, implemented, realized, recorded, monitored and evaluated?

3. In whose terms will relevance be discussed and decided?
4. How will discussions of relevance be managed?
5. How will the ground be laid for such discussions?

Curriculum issues

1. How up-to-date must the knowledge be in different areas of the curriculum?
2. How practical must the work be to ensure relevance?
3. In what terms will relevance be discussed (e.g. knowledge, concepts, skills, attitudes, areas of experience, regions of application, disciplines, subjects, pedagogies, ideologies, epistemologies, sociologies, organizations, school locations)?
4. How will the relationship be achieved between the logical structures of knowledge and the psychological frameworks of children's learning?
5. To whom, and to what, must the content be relevant?
6. In what terms will relevance be achieved across and through the school?
7. How will children be motivated?
8. How will relevance be balanced to differentiation?
9. How will relevance be decided in teacher-chosen and child-chosen curricula?
10. How will relevance enter the discussion of breadth and depth in currricula in relation to individual needs, interests and abilities?
11. How will relevance enter the discussion of balanced and unbalanced curricula?
12. How will knowledge be structured so that it is readily assimilated by children?
13. How specific or immediate to the school situation ought the curriculum content to be?
14. How will children's perceptions of relevance be ensured?

Differentiation

This notion encapsulates a central feature of primary education – its emphasis on the individual. For curriculum planners there are two main implications of this term. Either it can mean children learning and progressing at their own rates and in their own ways on predetermined tasks (where teachers operate from individual levels of demand, expectation and pedagogic styles (DES, 1985e)), or it can mean a child-chosen curriculum or part of a curriculum. Though HMI does not reach a decision on the alternatives, curriculum planners will have to address the issue, which has both ideological and organizational ramifications.

Planners will have to consider the relationship or balance between differentiation and the other terms from HMI, to decide how much increasing differentiation will decrease balance and breadth, how far the system can tolerate differentiation in children with special educational needs in mainstream classes or how far differentiation will lead to separation, and at what levels curriculum differentiation will apply — aims, objectives, content, pedagogy, evaluation criteria, and resources.

In evaluating the curriculum for differentiation planners could address the following questions.

Management issues

1. At what stages of planning should notions of differentiation enter the discussion?
2. How can teachers be prepared to observe and plan for differentiation?
3. How will differentiation be ensured across the year/school/schools?
4. How will differentiation be planned, managed, realized, recorded, implemented, monitored and evaluated?
5. In whose terms will discussions of differentiation be treated and decided?
6. How will notions of differentiation enter whole school discussion?

Curriculum issues

1. In what terms can differentiation be discussed (e.g. rates of learning, abilities of children, types of task — incremental, practice, revision, application, enrichment, problem-solving, investigational — interests and relevance, pedagogies, areas of experience, regions of application, disciplines of knowledge, subjects, ideologies, epistemologies, levels of thinking (low to high order), organizations and structures of the curriculum)?
2. Where should differentiation be sought?
3. How desirable an aim is differentiation?
4. What is the relationship of differentiation and common curricula?
5. How will the content be planned to ensure that it is interesting, stimulating, and motivating to children?
6. How will individual learning styles be accommodated?
7. How does the content embody the principles of the primary ethos?
8. How will planners ensure that the child perceives and appreciates differentiation?
9. How will the balance be struck between differentiation and uniformity?
10. How does the content develop types and levels of thinking—the cognitive demand on children?
11. How will the knowledge be structured and approached so that it is readily learnt by children?

12. In what terms will pupils' age, grasp and development of the content be assessed and evaluated?

Progression

Curriculum planning for progression will have to be approached at both a theoretical and a practical level. At a theoretical level planners will have to decide on the criteria for progression – what progression in knowledge, concepts, skills and attitudes really means; whether progression is quantitative, qualitative or both. While this may be comparatively straightforward in subject-based curricula or in areas where logical developments are clear (mathematics, for example), it is infinitely more difficult in integrated organizations or curricula or in skills-based teaching. How far, for example, can one plan for progression in topic work or study skills? Is progression simply the accretion of a number of skills, of should it be thought of in terms of levels of difficulty?

The problem with this latter criterion is that difficulty is specific to individuals. It is perhaps impossible to define levels of difficulty objectively (e.g. Goldstein's criticisms of the Rasch model for APU testing, in Lacey and Lawton, 1981. Similarly patterns of progression may vary for each child. Thus planning for progression involves planning for development at norm-related and individual-related levels. One can progress in many ways (Bloom, 1956; Wheeler, 1967; Waters, 1982; Wilson, 1983; DES 1985e):

- simple to complex;
- singular factor to multiple factors;
- generality to specific details;
- low order to high order;
- unique instance to overarching principle;
- specific to general;
- concrete to abstract;
- familiar to unfamiliar;
- contemporary to past and future;
- near to distant;
- abstract to concrete.

Many of these sequences are almost polar opposites; there being no single way of proceeding, planners have to debate and decide on the most appropriate ways of achieving progression, building on previous knowledge, concepts, skills and attitudes perhaps through the notion of the 'spiral curriculum' discussed earlier.

In evaluating progression, planners could address the following questions, arranged by management and curriculum issues.

Management issues

1. In whose terms will discussions of progression operate?
2. How will progression be planned, managed, realized, implemented, monitored, recorded and evaluated?
3. How will progression influence curriculum structure and staff deployment, e.g. generalism and subject specialist teaching?
4. How will the ground be laid for discussions of progression?

Curriculum issues

1. How will progression in integrated curricula be discussed?
2. In what terms will progression be discusssed (e.g. elements of learning, areas of experience, regions of applications, disciplines of knowledge, subjects, types of task (incremental, practice, revision, application, enrichment, problem-solving, investigational), rates of learning, levels of demand, low-order facts to high-order principle, quantitative and qualitative types of development)?
3. What are the constituents of progression in each curriculum area?
4. How far is progression quantitative (cumulative) or qualitative?
5. How can progression be systematized, sequenced and structured?
6. What is the relationship between logical sequences of content and psychological sequences in progression?
7. What is the relationship of progression and continuity?
8. What is the relationship of progression and differentiation?
9. How will planners ensure that the child perceives progression?

Continuity

Continuity is not concerned solely with transition periods, i.e. infant to junior, junior to secondary, first to middle, middle to upper; it is a concept which pervades the day-to-day implementation of the curriculum. Planners can strive for continuity in many forms; e.g. continuity of

- experience
- skills
- concepts
- knowledge
- attitudes
- in-school and out-of-school experiences

- pedagogy (across curriculum areas and through the school – vertical and lateral)
- organizations
- aims
- management styles
- ethos
- ideologies
- epistemologies
- key concepts
- assessment criteria and methods
- social experiences

At one level continuity of experiences can simply mean planning for flexible time boundaries so that children can work at their own rates until a task is completed. This is the principle embodied in the 'integrated day' form of organization, implementing the primary ethos very clearly. This reinforces the notion that continuity, like balance, must be perceived by the child as well as the planner.

At another level it involves planners in debating the areas in which continuity is to take place: how it will be implemented and monitored; what information will be passed and in what forms; what the relationship is between continuity and progression; whether there is a 'core' of areas in which continuity must be ensured; what the relationship is between continuity and common curricula; and how much continuity is desirable – whether times of 'planned discontinuity' (Tickle, 1985) might not have more merits than total continuity.

This latter point relates back to the discussion of commonality and individualism in curriculum planning and practice, to ask how far continuity reduces teacher autonomy and individuality. There is also the question of how far continuity will imply uniformity. It may be that children respond to – and look forward to – change, both in styles of teaching and organizations of curricula both across and through the curriculum (vertical and horizontal continuity, Blyth and Derricot, 1985). For example, at the time of primary to secondary transition, children may be seeking the different organizations of secondary schools. Primary schools can prepare children for this by some subject and specialist teaching for the older junior age range (Tickle, 1985). Teachers of top junior and early secondary children might also share the teaching in both schools, perhaps on a two-yearly cycle. The question then of the desirability of continuity is raised; at what point might conflict and discontinuity be more challenging and beneficial than continuity and total consensus?

By focusing on the issue of continuity, curriculum planners will have to address: the notions of coherence and consistency; the reduction of repetition of content (CACE, 1967); the need for whole school curriculum planning and policy making; the form, use and extent of formal record keeping; the problems of transition and liaison with other schools; the organization of knowledge; the problems of moving from integrated to separated curricula; and the dimensions of the curriculum along which it is to operate. It requires planners to identify and overcome barriers to continuity, which will involve the issues in the management of curriculum change (Dalin, 1978).

Continuity need not threaten individualism and autonomy; indeed, it may respect and build on it. Whole school planning and autonomy are not mutually exclusive.

Evaluation questions for Addressing Continuity

In attempting to evaluate the curriculum in terms of the continuity issue raised, planners could address the following questions which, for each characteristic, are grouped according to management and curricular issues.

Management issues

1. How will continuity be ensured across the year/school/schools?
2. What is the relation of continuity and teacher autonomy?
3. Who decides, and how is the decision reached, on where continuity will be?
4. How will continuity be planned, managed, realized, implemented, monitored, recorded and evaluated?
5. How will barriers to continuity be identified and overcome?
6. How will liaison and communication be ensured in discussions of continuity?
7. How will the climate of the school be set up and built so that discussions of continuity can proceed?
8. In whose terms will continuity be discussed and decided?
9. How far does continuity imply conformity and uniformity of beliefs and practices by teachers and pupils?

Curriculum issues

1. How much continuity is desirable?
2. Where is continuity desirable and undesirable?
3. In what terms will continuity be expressed (e.g. knowledge, concepts, skills, attitudes, experience, aims, ideologies, epistemologies, pedagogies, sociologies, in-school and out-of-school experiences, areas of

experience, disciplines of knowledge, regions of application, subjects, organizations, management styles)?
4. What is the relationship of continuity and consensus?
5. What is the relationship of continuity and common curricula?
6. How will content be structured to ensure continuity and progression?
7. How will continuity be ensured in the child's mind?

General

1. Select topic − criteria of relevance, integrative potential, declaration of curricular emphasis, non-contrivance, concrete
2. Brainstorm/read around/investigate
3. Organize by curriculum areas and cross-curriculum areas.
4. Note knowledge, concepts, skills, attitudes, activities for each area − at a general level
5. Sequence − a flow diagram − single or multistranded. Plan continuity, progression. Continuity of what? Progression of what? Decide criteria for the sequence − logical
                        − specific to general
                        − near to far
                        − concrete to abstract
                        − level of cognitive demand
                        − type of activity
6. Differentiate − what to differentiate
                  − how to differentiate
   Matching   − type of demand
                  − type of task
                  − level of demand
7. Decide appropriate teaching and learning styles for activities, children, stages of session:
                  − group, class, individual learning
                  − problem solving, investigational,
                          didactic, informal
8. Decide resources − first hand/second hand
                  − materials
                  − time
                  − space
                  − display
                  − internal/external environment
                  − staff
9. Plan how to introduce/develop/conclude/evaluate
10. How to set out in writing the individual sessions, specificity of detail, link of planning to evaluation.

Specific

FIGURE 6.9   A curriculum planning sequence

CONCLUSION

The discussion of the characteristics of the curriculum has shown that both within and between them there are tensions and conflicts which are exposed by considering the principles which make up the primary ethos. Curriculum planning for the selection and organization of content will need to resolve those tensions collegially, deciding on the paths to be taken through them. It points to the need for curriculum planning to be considered at a whole school level in a way which preserves the best of individualism; Figure 6.9 shows a curriculum planning sequence.

Autonomy and whole school planning are not mutually exclusive. In evaluating curriculum content, planners will have to bring to the debate the full range of issues and contexts brought out through the book. The content is the outcome of those discussions. The salutory comment of Chapter 2 — that the curriculum is what each child takes away — should remind planners that curriculum content must balance with the psychological make-up and learning styles of each child. The balancing of flexibility and novelty exacts a price; the curriculum planner and decision-maker must be constantly and acutely aware of the responsibility to provide a coherent, comprehensive, interesting and developed curriculum. To do this effectively requires effective evaluation of curricula and planning, which is the subject of the next chapter.

7
PLANNING CURRICULUM EVALUATION

In planning the curriculum, decision-makers will have to address the notion of evaluation; evaluation must be planned, for too often it is arbitrary, incidental or simply absent from the curriculum debate. While criteria for evaluating issues in the curriculum have been discussed as they appear throughout the book, planners will need to address the issues of evaluation *per se*. This chapter raises such issues and attempts to offer guidelines for planning the evaluation components of a curriculum. To do so the chapter will consider a variety of issues involved in planning an evaluation.

DEFINING EVALUATION

The causes of interest in curriculum evaluation have been set out in Chapter 1. Such interest, however, masks the conceptual problems which lie at the heart of curriculum evaluation, for the term is little more than a convenient label which can be attached to a vast and disparate group of concerns and practices. Consequently, in addressing evaluation curriculum planners must clarify its meanings, frames of reference, central issues, methodologies, purposes and practices. At a definitional level evaluation subsumes judgement, decision-making, assessment, appraisal and review – and yet is more than the sum of these parts. The differences can be teased out further.

'Review' indicates a retrospective examination or reflection on a curriculum or practice (Skilbeck, 1984; DES, 1985g) and participants' perspectives on it. 'Assessment' is a 'process of determining and passing judgements on students' learning potential and performance' (Skilbeck, 1984, p. 238); it involves measuring or grading students according to some agreed criteria; it assumes comparison of pupils either with each other (norm-referenced assessment) or individually with a specific standard (criterion-referenced assessment). On the other hand, 'appraisal' is less quantitatively or comparison-based; it leans towards qualitative judgements about the worth or value of an activity, organization or curriculum (DES, 1985g).

Evaluation has many interpretations which draw on review, assessment and appraisal. It can be seen as the 'collection and use of information to make decisions about the educational programme' (Cronbach, 1963); alternatively, a clearer valuative tone is struck by Cooper (1976) and Simons (1984): 'curriculum evaluation is the collection and provision of evidence, on the basis of which decisions can be taken about the feasibility, effectiveness and educational value of curricula' (p. 51). Evaluation, then, is about judgements of value on the basis of evidence. It also implies in its notions of valuing the need for debate, a point reinforced by Kemmis (1982), which underlines one of the central themes of planning which runs through the book: 'evaluation is the process of marshalling information and arguments which enable interested individuals and groups to participate in the critical debate about a specific programme' (p. 221).

In approaching evaluation and evaluating curriculum planning there are several issues which have to be resolved, regardless of the level of the evaluation − from national to institutional, and from internal to external, formal to informal, institutional to individual, evaluation by others to self-evaluation.

METAPHORS OF EVALUATION

When considering evaluation of the curriculum it is useful to consider the metaphors which planners and teachers use in describing the curriculum, for it reveals the ways in which that curriculum is perceived (House, 1986). Curricula may be perceived as machines, each element designed to fit with another to produce a pre-ordained outcome. Thus evaluation becomes a question of making the machine more efficient − altering the parts, oiling the workings and assessing the outcomes. Evaluation does not produce a radically new machine, hence the ideological commitment of this curriculum and evaluation is conservative and revisionist rather than reconstructionist.

Alternatively, curricula may be perceived as buildings (House, 1986) where a firm foundation has to be laid, where the construction has to be firmly planned, where the design has to be interesting and where cost analysis figures importantly. Evaluations thus are expected to be solid, well constructed (ibid.) and to yield information about the design, construction, utility, cost-effectiveness, aesthetic appeal, sequence and structure of the curriculum. Third, if one thinks of curricula as pipelines (ibid.) laid between aims and outputs, then importance attaches to their effectiveness in bringing about outcomes. How does the input lead to the outcomes? What contaminating or purifying curricular interventions occur during the course of the pipeline to produce the outcome? How can the pipeline be improved so that the outcomes do derive from the aims and objectives of the curriculum? How one thinks of evaluation affects the focus, purpose, methods and criteria for evaluating.

PURPOSE OF THE EVALUATION

Because of the many facets of evaluation at a conceptual level, any evaluation must be clear on its purposes as this will affect the sort of information sought, the judgements made, and the methods employed. In posing the question 'why evaluate?' two sorts of answers may be given. The question 'why?' is ambiguous, focusing on causes of evaluation and intentions of evaluation. Causes of evaluation may lie in economic funding decisions, accountability and political expediency; intentions of evaluation may be broader and more professionally oriented.

Eraut (1984) classifies purposes in a threefold manner: extrinsic, intrinsic purposes and value judgements. In 'extrinsic purposes' evaluation serves decision-making, accountability and assessment of learning; in 'intrinsic purposes' it examines the relation between intention and realization, it interprets what is happening, it ascribes value to intentions, actions and activities; in 'value judgements' evaluation concerns what is good, what has priority, and what is reasonable. More fully perhaps it is possible to itemize purposes of evaluation, some of which have already been introduced:

- to answer questions of selection, adoption and value of curricula and activities (Glass, 1975);
- to compare courses (Pope, 1983);
- to monitor standards (Taylor and Richards, 1979);
- to check progress (ibid.);
- to inform decision-making for course improvement (Cronbach, 1963);
- to demonstrate a promotion seeker's competence (Walker, 1981);

- to inform a funding decision (Taylor, 1976);
- to act as a public relations exercise (McCormick and James, 1983);
- to clarify roles and role relationships (Whitaker, 1983);
- to revitalize the institution and release energy for development (Nuttall, 1981);
- to clarify a school's philosophy and policy (ibid.);
- to maintain morale (ibid.);
- to facilitate informed comparison between schools (ibid.);
- to provide information for LEA and governors (ibid.);
- to clarify leadership patterns (Whitaker, 1983);
- to aid professional development (McCormick and James, 1983);
- to diagnose – to obtain feedback on curricula, teaching, students, activities, strengths and weaknesses (Eisner, 1979);
- to compare – programmes, teaching, school organization (ibid.);
- to improve school quality (ibid.);
- to anticipate educational needs (ibid.);
- to determine whether, and to what extent, objectives have been achieved (ibid.);
- to diagnose the initial state of the curriculum, pupils, teachers and organization (Glaser, 1977);
- to ascertain weaknesses in course provision (Pope, 1983);
- to meet accountability demands (McCormick and James, 1983);
- to determine the effectiveness of courses (Pope, 1983).

The purposes of the evaluation will illuminate the scope of the evaluation which can range from national levels (e.g. DES, 1974, 1978a, 1982b) to regional or school levels, from vast areas of the curriculum at a national level to education systems or whole school evaluation which cut across subject boundaries into policies and philosophies.

DEMAND FOR, AND AUDIENCES OF, EVALUATION

In considering the purposes of evaluation, the question has to be posed 'whose purposes does the evaluation serve?'; the origins of the demand for evaluation must be identified. House (1976), for example, contends

the context of the valuation involves the basic slant derived from the genesis of the evaluation, and includes all those motivations, biases, values, attitudes and pressures from which the evaluation arose...[and involves] problems of trying to determine the social worth of educational programs; valuation, justification, persuasion, values, thought, action, morality, knowledge, power.

(House, 1976, p. 12)

The identification of the origin of the demand for evaluation will involve ascertaining the reasons which the originators have for wanting the evaluation to be done (Harlen and Elliott, 1982). It will also denote the possible audiences of the evaluation (ibid.), e.g. LEA, parents, critics, governors, HMI, colleagues, course directors, planners, headteachers and other schools. The significance of these two factors lies in their ability to determine the level and type of information sought, the degree of involvement, exposure or honesty on the part of those being evaluated or participating in the evaluation, the formality or style of the report, and the credibility of the evaluation.

Eisner (1979) discusses such problems of writing evaluation reports as those of communicability – that the form of the report must be appropriate to the audience. For example, the demand from an adviser to produce an evaluation document on science teaching in a school for receipt by parents, governors and LEA, will very likely produce a different report from an evaluation of science teaching instigated by a non-scientist colleague wishing to find out how she or he can improve their own science teaching.

One may be factual, stating staffing, qualifications, curricula in their broadest sense, resources and perhaps examination results, whereas the other, if it is in report form at all, may contain analysis of strengths and weaknesses of the curriculum, its teaching strengths and weaknesses, unsupported opinion and judgement, and perhaps proposals to improve the quality of the curriculum and teaching. The former may be self-justificatory or bland, the latter – with a highly restricted audience and specific purpose – may be critical, honest and perhaps speculative.

The recipients of the evaluation will determine both what is included and how it is written up, for different audiences will have different backgrounds, perceptions, constraints on them and power to take action. This will influence the format of the report, from highly formal to informal. A highly formal report will be pitched at influential groups and the academic community (Walker, 1981), and adopt a weighty and academic style, with sophisticated evaluation instruments and clearly defined methodology. An informal report – pitched for a more general readership – will be written in everyday language, making no pretensions to a 'scientific' approach, and involving limited measurement techniques. At a level of medium formality, between the two extre. ies, a planned evaluation, aimed at interested parties and specified audiences, will use some data collection and treatment techniques even though these are relatively unsophisticated.

There is clearly a political aspect to the issue of the audiences of the evaluation; the evaluators and those evaluated will have to choose their allegiances or clarify the terms of reference unambiguously and unequivocally (MacDonald, 1982), recognize the limits to their autonomy, and recognize the potential threat to teachers which evaluation can pose (Adelman, 1984). Evaluation has a concomitant political dimension. In this respect MacDonald (1976) has outlined three forms of evaluation — bureaucratic, autocratic and democratic. The three characterizations hinge on the power of the evaluator and the power of the recipients of the evaluation to take action and decisions.

In bureaucratic evaluation the evaluators unconditionally serve those demanding the evaluation, providing information or recommendations which, once given, are out of their control or ownership — who pays the piper calls the tune. The controlling power demanding the evaluation can use the information as it wishes, and can accept or reject any recommendations made by the evaluators or the evaluation. In autocratic evaluation conditional service is given by the evaluator. Information and recommendations are made with which the receiving authority must comply; hence a measure of power and independence is controlled by the evaluator. In democratic evaluation the audience is wide, the evaluator is providing the whole community, however defined, with information; the report does not make recommendations or judgements, the community decides.

These three characterizations typify perhaps the proactive and reactive power that audiences of evaluation can have on the nature of the report. If teachers regard evaluation as a threat, inviting them to reveal their weaknesses, then natural reluctance in this respect is inevitable, particularly if the audiences could be condemnatory, powerful in determining career prospects or significant decision-makers on funding, resources and policies. For example, teachers will understandably be unwilling to divulge what they perceive to be their own weaknesses to a headteacher or adviser who a week later might be interviewing them for promotion or for filling a vacancy in a particular school or curriculum area. Certain types of information, then, can disadvantage some individuals, often those with little power (McCormick and James, 1983). The element of control of information must be approached.

ETHICS OF EVALUATION

If evaluation is politically non-neutral (Lawton, 1983) and the evaluators' roles vary, then the control of information collected must be established at the outset, for this clearly affects the types of information elicited. The ownership of information can affect the degree of frankness, bias, honesty or the amount of information provided by a subject. Procedures must therefore be established which will clarify the collection, ownership and release of information (Harlen and Elliott, 1982). At the heart of the control issue is a dichotomy between the public's and the evaluator's 'right to know' and the person's 'right to privacy' (McCormick and James, 1983). It is a problem too of the ethics of confidentiality; Pring (1984) sees this as a twofold problem. Initially if an evaluator has to present a report, for example, to a project director or head of department, then this may be exclusive, debarring those evaluated from seeing the final report, denying them accessibility (MacDonald, 1977). This cedes considerable power both to the evaluator and the recipients; the evaluator may be putting an interpretation in the report which unfairly reflects information from those evaluated or induces features not originally present. Second, the evaluator may be including material which was given in confidence, or given in the knowledge that clearance would be obtained it it were to be used or publicly broadcast − this is particularly true if the comments or opinions are unfavourable, personal or revealing immoral acts, e.g. stealing (McCormick and James, 1983).

In a report whose audience is exclusive the subjects may never know if their confidences have been respected; alternatively, in a report whose audience is wide the subjects may not wish certain comments to appear, particularly if the authorship could be traced without difficulty, be it teachers or children; anonymity may not be enough (Elliott and Adelman, 1976). Pring (1984) sets out five criteria which reconcile the dichotomy and which evaluators would negotiate before commencing evaluation:

1. The evaluator sets out the kinds of knowledge required.
2. The evaluator is open to cross-examination on the evaluation.
3. Information or opinion is treated confidentially, subject to clearance.
4. Interpretation of data is open to critical scrutiny by those evaluated.
5. The evaluator would provide reports which could be examined by those evaluated.

A final consideration in the ethics of evaluation is the profile of the evaluator − does the evaluator adopt an overt or covert style (McCormick and James, 1983), declaring intentions or keeping them unspoken? The latter may elicit information which otherwise may not be forthcoming; the former may elicit information in only a portion of the areas for investigation. Again, here the ethics of confidentiality are addressed and procedures which respect this have to be observed (e.g. Simons, 1982; Pring, 1984).

NATURE AND ROLES OF THE EVALUATOR

Initially this divides itself principally into two concerns: who the evaluators will be and what their roles are. In regard to the former, this concerns external and internal evaluators to a curriculum, school or project; which type is chosen depends on appropriacy to purpose. External evaluators, including teachers from other schools, HMI, heads, deputies, union representatives, staff from higher education institutions, professional consultants, representatives of professional associations, advisers and academics, can claim several strengths; they have the benefit of objectivity, possibly expertise in evaluation, and a view to broad perspectives and constraints in which a curriculum is located. However, they may be insensitive to the complexity or specificity of a curriculum in a particular school; they can also pose a threat to teachers. External evaluation can take the form of testing (e.g. the Assessment of Performance Unit (APU)), consultation, ethnographies, inspections of aspects of a school by national or local bodies, and formal evaluation with a variety of instruments.

Testing, while having the advantage of providing norm-referenced, quantifiable results, poses problems of representing education mechanistically, of being arguably invalid measures of education, of casting teachers in powerless positions – having no control over the tests and no rights of redress (McCormick and James, 1983), and of being of limited use in suggesting lines along which curriculum development can proceed. Inspections, though they may be superficial, impressionistic and susceptible to personal intervention by headteachers good at public relations, offer a more humane front than testing. It is a more flexible tool than testing, allowing for interpersonal relationships, and premissed on suggesting lines of development and improvement, i.e. having greater explanatory potential than testing.

The notion of internal evaluators – planners, headteachers, curriculum leaders, teachers – has many strengths (Davis, 1983). Such evaluators may have greater commitment to the evaluation and its outcomes; they will be aware of the subtleties and complexities of a particular school; they might have a considerable store of knowledge available to them by having been in the situation for some time. Further, their knowledge of personalities might enable them to elicit considerably more information and participation from staff than an outsider, perhaps because less of a threat is being posed. Against this however are several problems. Insiders may be too familiar with a situation (Eisner, 1985); they may miss significant but day-to-day activities; they may be unable to view matters objectively, whether they want to or not. Being caught up in a situation may prevent honest criticism from being formulated for fear of souring relations or articulating discordant values among staff. The interesting question raised here also is the ability of staff to evaluate each other: will an inexperienced colleague be capable of evaluating an experienced or inexperienced colleague, or will an experienced teacher be able to evaluate colleagues? The issue is raised by Eisner (1985) in his notion of 'connoisseurship' — an appreciation of the qualities of curriculum as practised:

> to be a connoisseur of wine, bicycles or graphic arts is to be informed about their qualities; to be able to discriminate the subtleties among types of wine, bicycles and graphic arts by drawing upon a gustatory, visual and kinaesthetic memory against which the particulars of the present may be placed for purposes of comparison and contrast.
>
> (Eisner, 1985, p. 92)

If a good teacher needs an awareness of the quality of a situation, activity, curriculum or pedagogy to be a connoisseur–evaluator, then the question is raised of the nature or length of teaching experience required for such a task: 'a teacher with years of experience in the classroom...might develop only enough educational connoisseurship to enable [her] to cope at minimal levels with the classroom and school in which they work' (ibid., p. 109). It also raises the question of who is to judge when a teacher is sufficiently experienced as a connoissuer to be able to act as an evaluator. Further, the critical factor of the credibility of the exercise is raised: internal staff may not have the expertise, time, status or legitimacy to perform the task with any measure of credibility. Walker (1981) suggests that of three levels of credibility of evaluators, teachers are ranked the lowest, the other two levels are external agents:

- Level one — high status — professors, university staff, researchers.
- Level two — medium status — college lecturers, LEA personnel.
- Level three — low status — teachers.

This low status or credibility afforded teachers need not mean, of course, that the evaluation is any less rigorous (McCormick and James, 1983), only that in terms of outsider interest it raises questions of validity.

It appears then that a mixed approach is perhaps appropriate, with insiders necessarily complementing outsider evaluation, and outsiders offering objectivity (triangulation) to insider evaluation; they are mutually supportive. In this too comes consideration of externally generated but internally administered evaluation schemes, where guidelines, purposes or foci are laid down perhaps at LEA or national level but interpreted, investigated and reported by schools, and internally generated but externally monitored evaluation schemes.

Given the complexity of the evaluation process it is necessary to determine the roles of the evaluator before the evaluation begins; clarity of conception at the beginning of an evaluation can anticipate and resolve problems of role definition. For example, the question will have to be decided, in advance of implementation, of whether or to what extent the evaluator can shape a curriculum plan or implementation, to make recommendations during the development of the curriculum, or whether the evaluator simply monitors and makes recommendations at the end (i.e. the extent of the evaluator's intervention). The timing of stages and foci here is crucial. Walker (1981) sees the evaluator as embodying several roles, suggesting perhaps that the notion of a single evaluator is better replaced with a notion of multiple evaluators. Roles can be described as: informer; judge; decision-maker; coordinator; report producer; consultant; collector of information; collator of information; monitor; or any combination of these. McCormick and James (1983) add to this the notion of 'critical friends' (be they external or internal evaluators), who have no authority position in relation to schools but have skills, expertise and well-founded relationships with teachers which can promote self-reflection and evaluation in a nonthreatening manner.

TIME SCHEDULE AND TIMING OF THE EVALUATION

The evaluation will have to consider time limits as these will determine feasibly what can and ought to be done in the time available. It will identify priorities and short- and long-term aspects of the evaluation. It will also draw attention to significant omissions occasioned by time constraints – some methods of evaluation take much longer than others. Second, the question of when the evaluation will be done must be addressed. Scriven (1967) suggests two types of evaluation timing: formative and summative evaluation. Formative evaluation takes place during the curriculum development and implementation, it is an ongoing process of monitoring, offering continuous feedback which may or may not shape the direction or course of the curriculum. Summative evaluation is terminal evaluation of the curriculum to ascertain the extent to which it fulfilled its objectives. Clearly, a full evaluation should embody both types; evaluation should be constant (Clemson, 1983). Harlen

(1971) expands this notion of ongoing evaluation by suggesting four stages at which evaluation should be done:

1. Stage one – evaluating the suitability of objectives.
2. Stage two – formative evaluation.
3. Stage three – evaluation of individual readiness and progress.
4. Stage four – summative evaluation.

This has resonances with Stake's (1976a) notion that antecedents, transactions and outcomes have to be evaluated; Stake puts this into a two-dimensional model which focuses on evaluating intended and observed curricula. Hence the evaluator gathers data on intended antecedents – what the planners intended there to be in the school before the new curriculum came into being. This is matched to the observed antecedents, what actually preceded the new piece of the curriculum, e.g. organization of learning, nature of pupil and teacher interactions, pupils' interests, environmental factors and teaching styles.

Alternatively, the intended antecedents might anticipate certain resources – equipment, time, staffing, money; this has to be matched to the level of resources observed before the new curriculum is implemented to ascertain where extra resources need to be provided. At the level of transactions the intentions can be compared to observed implementations, for example, to see if planned activities or learning situations or environments actually happened in the ways intended. Similarly, at the outcome stage the evaluator has to gather data on what outcomes were intended, e.g. knowledge, behaviour, skills, concepts and attitudes, and match them to the observed outcomes, what was actually learned or practised or acquired. This harks back to the earlier definition that 'the effective curriculum is what each child takes away' (Schools Council, 1981, p. 42). At all three levels Stake (1976a) suggests that a measure of congruence between intention and actuality is being sought. This goes back again to the notion raised in Chapter Two of matching rhetoric and reality, intentions and practice.

FOCUS OF THE EVALUATION

The issues raised so far point to the need for curriculum evaluators to be clear on the focus of the evaluation, be it persons, e.g. teachers and children, or practices, e.g. curricula, pedagogy, assessment procedures. The focus may well determine the methods of evaluation employed. Stake's foci have already been delineated; additionally, Eisner (1979) suggest three subject matters of evaluation – the curriculum, the teaching and the outcomes (Norris, 1975; Borich, 1977; DES, 1985c). These are dealt with throughout the book, covering:

- background constraints on the curriculum;
- ideologies, epistemologies, sociologies, cultures;
- aims;
- objectives;
- content;
- skills;
- evaluation and assessment procedures;
- management structures and styles;
- record keeping;
- resources and their utilization;
- the planning and preparation of the learning;
- the sequencing of the work;
- class management, organization and order;
- teaching styles and their variety;
- learning styles, individual differences and preferences;
- motivating children;
- rewards and punishments;
- skills in exposition, questioning, discussion and summary;
- pupil and teacher relationships.

Evaluation of outcomes will look for the match between what has been taught and what has been learnt – specific perhaps to children, teachers and the subject (Eisner, 1985). It is here that there is a strong potential threat to teachers, for attempting to evaluate teacher performance by pupil outcomes is fraught with problems as it slides over the sundry and significant features of pupils and their learning, which may be out of the teacher's control and for which teachers cannot be fully held morally accountable (Kelly, 1982). Gronlund (1974) gives these factors as:

- intelligence;
- past achievement;
- self-concept and self-knowledge;
- acceptance of school knowledge;
- school conditions, resources, ratios of teachers to children;
- out-of-school factors (socioeconomic), community environment;
- interaction of out-of-school and in-school factors

Further, such a model assumes that teachers are only concerned with products and neglect processes, which is a very narrow perspective on the curriculum and on education.

An alternative approach to evaluation, geared more towards self-evaluation, is offered by the Open University (1980) which suggests six main questions which curriculum evaluators may ask of themselves. The evaluation is geared totally to analysis, reflection and, significantly, to action — the characteristics perhaps of the reflective teacher as a model of good practice. For each question there are several contributory considerations. The scheme is presented in Table 7.1.

Given the variety of responses anticipated from these questions, and given the previous debate on effective teaching, the thrust of the implications is to throw into doubt the notion that consensus can ever be achieved other than at a superficial or general level on the constitution of effectiveness in any narrowly prescriptive sense. Effectiveness covers many variables; how total or partial must a teacher's possession of the many possible variables be in order to be judged effective? The term must be used relative to a situation, an individual child, teacher, curriculum or task. In establishing the focus of evaluation, then, the evaluator must be clear on the factors contributing to the particular situation being evaluated.

METHODS OF GATHERING EVALUATION DATA

Techniques of gathering data are not arbitrary; methods are selected on the criterion of appropriacy for eliciting the type of information required -- certain methods yield certain types of data. The criterion of appropriacy will have to take account of the purpose, focus, audience, role of the evaluator, model to be used (discussed later), timing and scale of the evaluation. Methods of gathering data lie along a continuum from quantitative to qualitative types; they can be represented in pairs thus (see also Stake, 1976b):

quantitative	qualitative
formal	informal
intermittent	long-term, continuous
objective	subjective
structured	unstructured
measuring	valuing
assessing	judging
describing	interpreting
looking at	looking for
preordinate	responsive
scientific	illuminative
statistical	ethnographic
deductive	inductive

TABLE 7.1   Open University questions for self-evaluation

1. What did the pupils actually do?
   (a) What did they do and what did they not do?
   (b) What I liked/disliked them doing?
   (c) How do I know what they were really doing?
   (d) What kind of evidence do I need to answer (c)?

2. What were they learning?
   (a) How do I know what they were really learning?
   (b) In what terms will I be looking, e.g. personal, academic?
   (c) How does what they were learning match up with my aims?
   (d) What might they have been learning?
   (e) How adequate were the opportunities for the learning? What were the contexts of their learning?
   (f) To what extent was learning actually taking place? Why do I need to know?
   (g) How can I assess it? (Type of evidence; comparing what the pupils do with whatever you think is appropriate.)
   (h) What have I learned from assessing the learning?

3. How worthwhile was it?
   (a) In what terms will I answer this? Overall or context-specific? Short-term/medium-term/long-term?
   (b) How explicit will you make your values?
   (c) In what terms will you judge the worthwhileness (pupils, teachers, etc)?
   (d) What assumptions are you making in your judgements?
   (e) How will you collect and analyse data to answer (c) and (d)?

4. And what did I do?
   (a) How fitting was it to the task?
   (b) How will I discuss it − in terms of planning, organizing, resourcing my role during the lesson, evaluation?
   (c) How will I find out what I did?
   (d) What evidence/whose evidence will I use to answer (c)?
   (e) At what level will I answer − general or specific?
   (f) What is the difference between my aims and my practices?

5. What did I learn?
   (a) Did I learn anything? Why not?
   (b) What did I learn about? Myself, the children, the activity, the subject, teaching and learning styles?
   (c) What did I learn about what the children did? What they were learning, how worthwhile it was, what I did? My behaviour with children? My role? My involvement?
   (d) What evidence do I need to answer?

6. What do I intend to do now?
   (a) How will the questions and answers to questions 1 to 5 affect my plans?
   (b) How will I answer questions 1 to 5 for my curriculum development?

nomothetic....................................idiographic
positivistic.....................................interpretive

Clearly, these parts are not discrete; nor need an evaluation draw on one type of data exclusively. An eclectic approach will use both quantitative analysis (figures, statistics and structured interviews or questionnaires) and qualitative data (opinions, perspectives and depth of response evoked), establishing concurrent validity of the evaluation by using a multi-method approach. Further, no method or type of method is objectively or intrinsically better than another, they are simply different, having their own strengths and weaknesses. For example, while quantitative analysis has the respectability of scientific procedures and can ostensibly measure factors, relationships and their subtleties with a high degree of systematic precision, Ruddock (1981) criticizes statistical methodology for combining 'great refinement of process with crudity of concept' (p. 49) – that the need to operationalize a concept demeans it or fails to encompass all its facets.

Similarly, Eisner (1985) criticizes quantitative methodologies for failing to distinguish between educational and statistical significance. However, qualitative methods, while possessing and reflecting immediacy, flexibility, authenticity and comprehensiveness, have been criticized for being impressionistic, biased, ungeneralizable, idiosyncratic, subjective and short-sighted. In short validity attaches itself differently according to the methods employed (Ruddock, 1981). Given these considerations, evaluators have at their disposal a battery of techniques available for gaining particular types of information: observation; testing; interviews and conversations; questionnaires; rating scales; records (field notes, documents, diaries); group discussions; children's work; reports; appraisal and self-appraisal schedules; personal constructs; Delphi techniques; nominal group techniques; sound and video recordings; photographs; profiles.

It is beyond the scope of this book to discuss each method and its handling in any depth; rather the discussion here briefly illustrates the nature and uses of five key methods – observation, interview, questionnaire, testing and records – revealing their potential for evaluation and their strengths and weaknesses.

Observation (both auditory and visual) is a key method for gathering information and feedback about curricula and children; it is probably the method most used by teachers on a day-to-day basis. It ranges from formal to informal, highly structured to unstructured. Structured observation works on an observation schedule of categories to be completed during the observation period. It might involve time sampling where a record is entered on the schedule of what is observed at fixed regular intervals, e.g. every five, ten or thirty seconds. Alternatively, it might involve event sampling (or sign systems) where a mark is entered in the appropriate category every time a particular event is observed in a given period, for example the child writing, or standing up, or walking around. One-zero sampling requires a mark to be entered in the appropriate category not every time it is observed but just once if it is observed. While event and one-zero sampling can yield frequencies of behaviours, they cannot provide the temporal order in which the behaviour occurred – they aggregate but do not sequence. On the other hand, time sampling has this potential for temporal sequencing, an important factor in tracking a child's behaviour or attempting to trace the causes or developments of a behaviour.

While structured observation clearly operates in a systematic and rigorously analytical manner and presents a wealth of numerical data which can be used to compare children, teachers and curricula, it presents several telling problems, both practical and theoretical. At a practical level the construction of an unambiguous schedule which exhaustively or adequately embraces all the aspects of the construct under investigation is extremely time-consuming, often requiring trial usage to refine the schedule and to ensure that if a team of evaluators is to use it, that there is parity in the way in which behaviours observed are entered in the categories. Further, the possibility of using it to study more than a handful of children at a time is restricted.

At a theoretical level the whole notion of structured observation has been questioned for its inability to take account of each participant's unique perception of a situation; it can only measure observable behaviour rather than intentions and thoughts (Stubbs and Delamont, 1976). Moreover, structured observation focuses on parcels or potentially disjointed fragments of behaviour, neglecting a more holistic view of what is occurring in the classroom. The use of prespecified categories is questionable (ibid.) as this prejudges what the observer will observe, which may only be a poor or partial record of what is actually taking place, i.e. they assume the truth of what they claim to be explaining. Category systems take continual still pictures of interaction and behaviour; they freeze behaviour, however momentarily. The validity of such a static approach to measuring a fluid, ever-changing active world of behaviour has to be questioned.

Unstructured and semi-structured observation, on the other hand, moves away from categories and schedules towards assessing and understanding the quality of a situation as a whole, hence the observer here (the participant–observer or observer-as-participant perhaps) does not enter the situation with predetermined notions of what to observe, but responds to the situation, allowing key issues and behaviours to present themselves, picking up the flavour of the situation. This requires a lengthy stay in the situation (often measured in months rather than hours). The observer records as much as possible in field notes – comprehensive personal records of behaviour, opinions, perceptions, reactions and understanding – then sifts through the data to decide on the key features, checks with the participants or a neutral party that they are in fact significant, and, sensitized to central issues, investigates these further by observation, the procedure of 'progressive focusing' (discussed later).

By staying in a situation for a considerable time the observer-effect is reduced, participants become used to the observer; the potential for observing more 'natural' behaviour rather than the 'staged' behaviour observed perhaps in brief periods of structured observation is greatly enhanced. Unstructured and semi-structured observation can be used as a complement to interviews, discussions and other means of data gathering; the data of all these other forms comprising the 'field notes' mentioned above. It underscores the model of 'illuminative evaluation' discussed later. It claims greater potential than structured observation for understanding classroom processes and explaining why situations operate in the way that they do.

Interviews, be they with individuals or groups, can, like observation methods, be highly structured, semi-structured or unstructured. A highly structured interview will have very specific questions requiring specific answers, perhaps of the multiple-choice or yes/no types; the same questions are given to all respondents. The advantage of a highly structured situation is that it provides many responses to the same question – a suitable basis for fair comparative analysis statistically. A completely unstructured interview has no predetermined areas of interest, it is more like a conversation, with the interviewer following the train of thought of the interviewee in an unforced, natural manner; hence in retrospect the interview may prove useful or useless in providing data. Data gathered is generally recorded after the event.

Between these two poles lies the semi-structured interview, where the interviewer has a checklist of items to be addressed, but phrases questions to suit the respondent, tailors the interview sequence to follow the natural flow of the respondent's conversation or thoughts rather than being bound to an immutable order, and asks open-ended questions which allow a free and full response. In these the value placed on the response lies in the 'candour, depth and richness of the information given. The more involved the respondent becomes in his account, and the deeper the level from which his answer springs, the more genuine and valid his responses will be' (Oppenheim, 1966, p. 76).

The semi-structured interview, then, is a useful instrument for covering the issues to be investigated in a manner which is sensitive to specific situations and which respects the individuality of each respondent. The problems which attach themselves to semi-structured interviews are twofold. First, in rephrasing questions, the basis for comparison of respondents' answers is reduced; they are different questions and may be interpreted differently. Further, the answers may be given out of anxiety to please or to say something rather than nothing, or may reflect what happens to be in the respondent's mind at the time rather than a fully considered response. All these features are particularly hazardous if interviewing children. Morever the intonation or phrasing of the question might be given or taken as a clue to the type of response sought. Simons (1982a) offers a useful set of considerations for evaluators approaching interviewing:

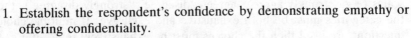

1. Establish the respondent's confidence by demonstrating empathy or offering confidentiality.
2. Respond acceptingly.
3. Allow the respondent to shift from topic to topic.
4. Accept unsolicited responses.
5. Be prepared to listen.
6. Use cues from the respondent to probe for depth.
7. Avoid asking too many questions.
8. Avoid accepting the initial response too readily.
9. Avoid summarizing erroneously.
10. Be socially responsive.
11. Recognize the need to be assertive if the respondent is being too repetitive.
12. Look for nonverbal cues.
13. Plan the order of interviewing candidates.
14. Note the number and kind of interruptions accepted during the interview.

Simons (1982a) also identifies problems associated with interviewing children:

1. How to avoid being seen as an authority sympathizer.
2. How to keep the interview relevant and focused.
3. How to avoid summarizing too early.
4. How to get the teacher out of the room.

5. How to interview inarticulate pupils.
6. How to respond to the person who reveals all and immediately wishes he had said nothing.
7. How to evoke pupil responses which are not just responses to the interview situation.
8. How to get beyond the institutional response in a short time.
9. How to avoid only the headteacher's view.
10. How to deal with reticent pupils.

The interview, then, is a powerful and flexible tool for eliciting data. It can reveal participants' motives, opinions, perspectives, reactions, explanations, thoughts and understandings of situations, all of which benefit the evaluator, be it an external agent or the teacher in the school.

Questionnaires may be regarded in some ways as interviews written down, for they too vary from the structured to the semi-structured, allowing for highly structured dichotomous or multiple-choice questions or those requiring a free response. If employing rating scales or Likert scales (e.g. 'strongly agree', 'agree', 'disagree', 'strongly disagree'), then the categories must be both exhaustive and exclusive. If multiple-choice questions are used then the choices must be exhaustively realistic, i.e. to represent the response with which the respondent can identify. Hence extremely careful devising and phrasing of questions is necessary, which may require a pilot stage.

While questionnaires have potential for supplementing interview or observation data, their inability to offer explanations, clarifications or probes renders them perhaps a weaker tool than the former two methods. There is no way of checking the depth of an attitude or opinion expressed in a questionnaire. There is a tendency for respondents using rating scales to avoid the extreme categories. There is difficulty in identifying how respondents interpret the anchor statements or categories in rating scales, hence the validity of questionnaires may be questionable. Questionnaires used to gather facts may be useful, those used to gather opinion are problematic – though perhaps not insuperably so.

Testing yields data on outcomes, performances and products, which are useful to an evaluator to gauge the success or appropriacy of objectives, programmes and pupils – be they norm-referenced or criterion-referenced tests. They have the clear strength of being objective, controlled, perhaps standardized, susceptible to statistical analysis, and useful for providing data for comparisons. This must not be allowed to cloud the problem of assessment in certain fields, for example, the affective or creative, where a mark is perhaps a crude measure of performance. Like structured observation or structured interviews, their explanatory potential is limited –

they only tell an evaluator *that* certain products were occasioned, not why. Similarly, they do not measure all the variables operating upon children's performances which are out of the teacher's control and which cause or constrain a particular outcome.

Records (documentary, formal, field notes or diaries, or informal records) are a valuable data source. Documents can comprise the range of written records, e.g. minutes of meetings, tests results, record of profile forms, briefing papers, syllabi, reports, notes or casual observations. Diaries kept by teachers, children or evaluators can record over time data from observations, interviews, questionnaires, or opinions, thoughts, perceptions, feelings, reactions, or facts about curricula and their implementations. They are flexible and open-ended, and if they are comprehensive and structured they can provide invaluable information either to corroborate, illuminate or explain situations or to suggest factors which may not be forthcoming to an evaluator.

Record-keeping informs evaluation and subsequent curriculum planning and decision-making. There are several issues in the devising, keeping and use of records which have to be addressed. Records offer data on which formative and summative evaluation are based. They will differ according to their intended audiences, purposes, format and coverage of curriculum areas: a personal record may be qualitatively different from a stylized record produced for a child's career through the primary school; and a mathematics record could well differ in form from a language record. Decisions have to be taken by curriculum planners on the monitoring of their curricula; these can be approached by addressing key questions.

What are the purposes of record keeping?

As well as informing planning, records serve a variety of purposes, as follows:

1. To record the achievement of children and teachers.
2. To record the experiences of children and teachers.
3. To record children's development.
4. To compare children.
5. To record progress and rates of progress.
6. To ensure coverage of the curriculum.

Seen in these lights, records cover intentions, implementation or transactions, and outcomes − which has resonances with Stake's (1976a) countenance and portrayal models of evaluation, outlined later. The School's Council (Clift, Weiner and Wilson, 1981 pp. 22-3) offers a comprehensive list of seven principal functions of record keeping in primary schools:

1. To supply information, to inform the day-to-day planning of the teacher. These could be, for example, running records of attainment and progress in reading, mathematics or language development.
2. To provide summary information to accompany pupils on their transfer from one teacher to another in school. These may be half-termly, termly, half-yearly or yearly.
3. To provide summary information to accompany pupils on their transfer from one stage to another or from one school to another. These may include:
   (a) nursery to infant or first school;
   (b) infant or first school to junior or middle school;
   (c) junior or middle school to secondary school.
4. To provide summary information to accompany pupils on their transfer from one school to another, other than for transition reasons. These could be for geographical moves or for changes within an area brought about for other reasons.
5. To diagnose pupil needs, progress, strengths and weaknesses.
6. To provide information for, or from, supporting welfare services, for example, school medical, psychological or social services.
7. To provide information for parents: these may be in the form of termly or yearly reports or records discussed at open evenings.

The format and information provided on records, then, will vary according to the purposes for which they are being kept.

What are the types of records?

A teacher wishing to plan appropriate curricula will draw on a variety of records. While there is a wealth of types of records they can perhaps be grouped thus:

1. Records of content covered, be they by lists, descriptions, flow charts, web diagrams or other forms.
2. Class records — a teacher's weekly record book under various headings is indicative of this type.
3. Summary records — infrequent reports detailing outline information only.

4. Individual pupil record cards, be they formal or informal, where the teacher notes pupil development in detail (in the form of daily, weekly, monthly, half-yearly or *ad hoc* comments).
5. Pupils' self-completion records, where children themselves mark off stages reached, books read, assignments completed, etc. These are the substance of recording in SRA and Reading Workshop laboratories and some mathematics schemes.
6. Teachers' records of group work completed or attempted.
7. Samples of children's work.

While such a list may or may not be exhaustive, it does signal a major problem in record-keeping — that it can easily go out of hand and become a time-consuming occupation undertaken merely for its own sake. This clearly is of limited value; records must be useful. The types of record link to the further question of the forms or formats of records. A teacher can draw on a variety of means of recording information:

1. Record of marks and results of standardized tests.
2. Personal observations.
3. Ticks against statements.
4. Rating scales against statements.
5. Marks against understanding of concepts and skills.
6. Multiple-choice questions.
7. Open-ended areas for comment.
8. Graphs, charts and histograms.
9. Photographs, film, video, slides, audio cassettes.
10. Flow charts and descriptions.
11. Records of significant behaviours or comments by children.
12. Check lists.

Criteria of appropriacy and usefulness clearly operate in selecting which of these methods to use. The reflective teacher will draw eclectically on these to suit purposes most efficiently.

What areas are covered by records?

While to do justice to the primary ethos outlined in Chapter 1, the whole personality, capability, experiences and all-round development of the child should be recorded (Sharp *et al.*, 1975), in reality the audiences of the records may well determine the answer to this question, as will the formality of the detail required. This ranges from the standard profile card kept by the school for every child, to the working records which teachers keep. Clift *et al.* (1981) found that teachers in the two hundred schools surveyed kept records of the areas shown in Table 7.2. The list is useful in drawing attention to the curricular, personal and social areas which records usefully cover. Again the striking problem is the scope and range of record keeping; too easily it can become an end in itself, exhausting and relatively valueless.

Given such scope the curriculum planner will have to weigh the merits and demerits which attach themselves to questions of record keeping. That they can be time-consuming is clear, hence ease of completion should be the goal. This brings problems in its wake, for while quickly completed tick sheets may reduce the time spent, a standardized format may not reflect an individual's specific profile nor the particular classroom organization and pedagogic styles which obtain in the classroom – a team teaching, open plan or integrated day situation may require a different recording system from a more traditional organization where one teacher works with one class.

Further, there is a tension between comprehensive and unnecessary detail, between specificity and generality. Tilting too far towards comprehensiveness may lead to a plethora of demanding records, many of which will serve little real or enduring purpose for the curriculum planner. On the other hand, too general a record can lead to platitudinous comments

TABLE 7.2   Records kept by teachers in the study by Clift *et al.* (1981)

Record	Percentage of teachers recording in the area
Reading development	96
List of maths topics covered	81
Social and personal development	55
Writing development (handwriting, spelling, syntax, expression)	35
Oral language development	34
Physical development (and medical notes on visual, auditory, health or motor problems)	31
Concept attainment in mathematics	29
Scientific skills and experiences (areas of study, topics, equipment used)	17
Aesthetic development and craft	14
Study skills	3

(Source: Clift *et al.* (1981) *Record Keeping in Primary Schools*, p. 14)

or risk unhelpful personal bias. Further, a general grade of C in English may obscure the fact that a child may be excellent in imaginative writing but appalling at spelling or punctuation – the usefulness of highlighting the extremes may be lost in an average.

A final tension exists between the alleged objectivity of the tick sheet and the subjectivity of the personal comment. Erring too far from a balance between the two poles can distort records into statistics or anecdotes. While they both have their place an appropriate balance must be struck between them. For the curriculum planner a record must be parsimonious, comprehensive, easy to keep, appropriate to the audiences and purposes, provide opportunity for balancing objective measures with subjective comments, and above all useful, being a springboard to action rather than a monument to pedantry.

With many methods available to evaluators the guiding principles should perhaps be appropriacy and eclecticism in selecting which evaluation techniques to employ. If quantitative and comparative analysis is deemed necessary then structured and formal approaches may be appropriate; if qualitative analysis is required then less structured approaches may be preferable, still maintaining rigour and methodological stringency (Huberman and Miles, 1984). However, the two have been demonstrated to be neither discrete nor exclusive (ibid.). The teacher and evaluator investigating an issue may find it beneficial to draw on many methods yielding many types of data. This attempts to ensure content and concurrent validity to the evaluation; to explore the full spectrum of concerns in an issue requires a full spectrum of methods.

SEQUENCING THE EVALUATION

In approaching curriculum evaluation and taking account of the issues raised, it is possible to suggest a possible sequence of a curriculum evaluation. Eraut (1984) offers a three-stage model: initiation, collection of evidence, and processing and reporting of information. Under 'initiation' one can include (Brink, 1983; Harlen and Elliott, 1982; Harlen, 1983; Eraut, 1984):

- considering the language and metaphors of evaluation;
- compiling an agenda of issues;
- deciding on the type of evaluation – formative to summative;
- deciding the purposes of the evaluation, what it is hoped it will achieve;
- deciding the criteria for the evaluation;

- deciding the focus of the evaluation;
- deciding the audience of the evaluation;
- deciding on the kind of evidence sought;
- deciding on the sources of the evidence;
- deciding on the methods to be used to gather evidence;
- deciding on the constitution, roles, power and responsibilities of the evaluator(s);
- deciding on the executive powers and roles of the audience of the evaluation;
- agreeing the ownership of the evidence;
- agreeing people's rights to gain or prevent access to evidence;
- deciding on the resources required for the evaluation — time, money, administrative support;
- deciding on methods to achieve reliability and validity of data collection and results;
- deciding on the form of the presentation and communication of the evaluation results;
- deciding on the form of the evaluation report;
- deciding on the use of the evaluation report to achieving the expressed purposes of the evaluation;
- deciding on the time scale and timing of the evaluation;
- deciding on the standards and criteria to be used to evaluate and judge the evaluation;

Under 'collection of evidence' will be methods, methodologies, manageability and participants' perceptions of the evaluation and the evaluators' roles.

In processing and reporting the evidence there is a clear need to link evaluation to action (Eraut, 1984), hence the necessity to have previously clarified the nature of the action or intervention of the evaluator, the report and its recipients.

MODELS OF EVALUATION

Curriculum planners and evaluators have diverse purposes and interests. In an attempt to articulate such diversity covered by the term 'evaluation', it is useful perhaps to consider models of curriculum evaluation. Planners can use models to clarify their thinking and to identify issues which surround different conceptions of the evaluation act. Such models will vary according to different evaluation criteria; Lewy (1977), for example, suggests that differences among evaluation studies may be classified under six issues:

1. The developmental stage of the programme − planning to implementation.
2. The entity to be evaluated − components or the whole.
3. Criteria for the evaluation, e.g. outcomes, processes, knowledge.
4. Data type, e.g. judgement, observation, records, interview data.
5. Mode of data summary − quantitative, qualitative.
6. Role of evaluation − formative, summative, for selection or modification or feedback on a programme.

Given such variables, six main models can be described, selected because they interpret the above issues in different ways which planners may find useful.

1. The objectives-based model

This has its focus on outcomes, the intention of the evaluation being to ascertain how far children have achieved prespecified objectives. It owes its pedigree to Tyler (1949) and his predecessors, and to Bloom (1956). This model exists to detect discrepancies between intended and observed outcomes. While it has the claimed advantage of objectivity, quantitative assessment and precise specification of the focus of the evaluation, it has the disadvantages of assessing and measuring without explaining why children or activities are proceeding in observed ways; it offers only limited feedback. Further, it neglects processes in favour of products, and risks an oversimplification of curriculum aims and objectives as they have to be specified and measured behaviourally (see the discussions earlier of objectives-based curriculum planning).

2. Classical research model

This is similar to the 'objectives' model and is often called the agricultural−botanical model (Lawton, 1980), indicating its origins. The seeds are pre-tested (e.g. weighed or measured) then sorted into two groups, one experimental group which will receive new different treatments and a control group which will not receive the new treatments, e.g. receiving different types or amounts of fertilization. Subsequently, the experimental and control groups are weighed or measured to compare the relative efficiency of the experimental group with the control group.

Applying the analogy to education, the curriculum planner would pre-test two groups of children – the control and the experimental groups – teach the new piece of the curriculum, re-test the groups and compare the relative advantage or progress of the two groups. While this model appears to possess the attraction of scientific respectability and specificity of analysis, there are difficulties with it. Initially the applicability of a model from agriculture or botany to human behaviour is questionable on practical and ethical grounds, smacking of engineering (Lawton, 1983). Human behaviour is not able to be isolated and controlled like plant behaviour; even if this were possible in laboratory conditions it would ignore the discrepancy between the artificial world of the laboratory and real life which contaminates subjects – regardless of the ethical problems of such laboratory research.

Moreover, the post-test would have limited validity; the control group not having been exposed to the new curriculum, it would be inappropriate to administer to them a test of that new curriculum – they would be certain to perform less well than the experimental group. Alternatively, if it were that the new curriculum offered only a different approach for the experimental group to learn the same content (however framed) as the control group, then this assumes, first, that curriculum projects undergo little or no change during the period of study – a premise rarely upheld in practice (Parlett and Hamilton, 1976) and, second, that variables other than the ones investigated are inoperable for both groups. It may be, for example, that the very fact of being in an experiment or being investigated will have an effect on motivation or performance (the Hawthorne effect). Such a model leans towards quantitative analysis – measures and figures – which may or may not describe the outcome of a curriculum, but which certainly explains very little about why the outcomes were what they were, i.e. it is of limited use to a planner.

3.   Illuminative model

In contrast to the two previous models the concern of the illuminative evaluator is with 'description and interpretation rather than measurement and prediction' (Parlett and Hamilton, 1976). It seeks to illuminate a curriculum in a particular school context experienced by specific teachers and children; in short, to discover the 'learning mileau' (ibid., p. 90). It strives to discover, understand and document what is happening, why it is happening, and participants' perspectives on the programme. Hence the evaluator attempts to reach inside the group under study, to illuminate the context from within rather than without, to gain as many different perspectives as possible on the curriculum.

Evaluators begin with a broad data base from observations, conversations, interviews, background sources, opinions, and attempt to clarify the central issues in the curriculum as it is experienced by the participants. They do not, then, approach the evaluation with predetermined items for investigation, rather they are responsive to the unique situation or context. By 'progressive focusing' − clarifying, redefining and further investigating what emerge as key issues − evaluators go through a three-stage process of observing, inquiring further and then seeking to explain the curriculum (Parlett and Hamilton, 1976). Such 'progressive focusing' reduces the problem of data overload experienced at the outset of the evaluation. It also has built-in checks for internal validity, for the evaluator presents back the findings to the participants to ensure that a fair interpretation is being given.

Validity is sought through 'triangulation', by seeking as many views as possible on a situation, e.g. teachers', children's, evaluators', and by employing a variety of methods to yield data on central issues, i.e. to provide concurrent validity. By being involved in the situation over a long period of time, and seeing participants in a variety of situations, the evaluator can construct perhaps a more valid picture of the curriculum as practised in a school than can a spasmodic series of short tests, questionnaires or interviews. The strength of this approach lies in the authenticity of the account which it can produce, and the acknowledgement of the significance of the context, interpersonal relationships and unique characteristics of a situation. These can be regarded as weaknesses, for the level of subjectivity is high, the generalizability is low, the sample tends to be small, and until recently only limited legitimacy has been accorded to qualitative measures.

Further, the nature of some of the evidence for the evaluation may be questioned (Simons, 1984); what will constitute adequate evidence, an uninformed or unsubstantiated value judgement, for example? Perhaps then the illuminative evaluator sacrifices a measure of objectivity and precision of measurement to comprehensiveness, understanding and depth of response.

4. Countenance or portrayal model

This model seeks to utilize features of both ends of the quantitative to qualitative continuum exposed in the preceding three models. It derives from Stake (1976b) who argues that evaluation, in seeking to report different perspectives on a curriculum, must refer to three distinctions: formal and informal analysis, description and judgement data, and analysis and portrayal. His model then is eclectic; it synthesizes elements from other models into a new framework.

Formal analysis is recognized by reliance on schedules and quantitative analysis, observation and interview, structured analysis, measurement and testing, while informal analysis dwells on qualitative analysis, opinions, perspectives, semi- or unstructured observation and description. Stake recommends both approaches as appropriate in his countenance model.

With regard to description and judgement data, both of which have a place in the model, Stake argues for describing and judging data on antecedents, transactions and outcomes (already discussed) in terms of the match between intention and observation. To make a full judgement it is necessary to gather the accounts from five groups of people — spokespersons for society at large, subject matter experts, teachers, parents, children. This, it is argued, will offer a true reflection of the pluralism of values present in a situation. For a full countenance of the evaluation, Stake suggests that evaluators should address five questions:

1. Is this evaluation to be primarily descriptive, primarily judgemental or both descriptive and judgemental?
2. Is this evaluation to emphasize the antecedent conditions, the transactions, or the outcomes alone, or a combination of these, or their functional contingencies (i.e. their interrelationship and associated factors)?
3. Is this evaluation to indicate the congruence between what is intended and what occurs?
4. Is this evaluation to be undertaken within a single programme or as a comparison between two or more curricular programmes?
5. Is this evaluation intended more to further the development of curricula or to help choose among available curricula?

(Stake, 1976b, p. 39)

In analysis and portrayal the question is one of focus. Does the evaluator focus on the curriculum as a whole or on parts of the curriculum — should one attend to the fine grain or to the grand sweep (Stake, 1976b, p. 40)? Stake argues that either components are analysed — objectives, environment, interaction, perceptions, accomplishments — or an overall view is taken, describing and interpreting rather than measuring and predicting, the whole being greater than the sum of the parts. It is impossible, he claims, to do both, as attention to analysis 'distorts the picture as to what the programme is' (Stake, 1977a, p. 161). Analysis and portrayal are, he argues, alternatives of equal status.

Goal-free model of evaluation

In this model, formulated by Scriven (1967) the evaluator 'deliberately avoids learning the objectives of the program, which frees him to assess its actual effects. . . . If intended effects are being achieved they should catch his attention' (Taylor, 1976, p. 356). The evaluator then studies the transacted curriculum unhampered by knowledge of the planner's intentions; this enables her or him to itemize significant or peculiar features of a school's curriculum, which then can highlight descrepancies between the perspectives of the planners and the users. To ensure that complete randomness is avoided the evaluator has a checklist of thirteen items which provide the basis of the enquiry − significant features allegedly necessary in any coherent curriculum − e.g. need, market, cost-effectiveness. The checklist thus represents a form of quality control. Hence absences or neglected areas can be identified.

The strengths of this approach lie in their potential comprehensiveness and their ability to release the evaluator from hide-bound adherence to curriculum planners' objectives. The principal weakness lies in the assumption that curricula can be fully evaluated by checklists, and that varieties of curricula can be evaluated by the same single checklist. With such strong criticisms this model is perhaps best used as an adjunct to other models.

Decision-making model

Teachers and curriculum planners are caught up in the web of decision-making for which information has to be provided (c.f. Cronbach's definition of evaluation (1963)). Decisions are informed by different types or foci of evaluation, the context of the decisions, and the type of decisions appropriate to that context. An attempt to synthesize this has been made by Stufflebeam (1976) who suggests four foci of evaluation: context, input, process and product evaluation.

Context evaluations, like situational analyses, identify perceived needs and problems underlying those needs, objectives and the operating context of the curriculum so that decisions can be reached on the setting of the curriculum (Wiles and Bondi, 1984). Input evaluations assess system capabilities − the strategies feasible for achieving the goals. These evaluations inform decisions on procedural designs, sources of support and strategies appropriate to the context. Process evaluations are intended to monitor the implementation of the strategies to detect defects and to inform decisions on refining, controlling and redesigning the curriculum. Product evaluation seeks information on outcomes to determine the match to intentions, goals, objectives, strategies and implementation, so that decisions can be taken to continue, terminate or refocus the curriculum.

Implicit in Stufflebeam's conception is a means−end model of curriculum

TABLE 7.3 Models of curriculum evaluation

Model	Purpose	Focus	Timing	Methodology
Objectives	Assessing achievement of objectives	Objectives and behavioural outcomes	Summative	Quantitative
Classical research	Measuring gains under controlled conditions	Initial state and outcomes	Pre-test and post-test	Quantitative
Illuminative	Description and understanding of a context-specific curriculum	Participants' and evaluators' perspectives on the curriculum and emerging key issues. The whole curriculum	Formative and summative	Qualitative
Countenance and portrayal	Reporting different perspectives on the curriculum	Participants' perspectives on the curriculum	Formative and summative	Quantitative and qualitative
Goal-free	Objective assessment of effectiveness of the curriculum	The observed curriculum	Formative and summative	Quantitative and qualitative
Decision-making	Curriculum decision-making	Contexts, inputs, processes	Initial appraisal. Formative and summative	Quantitative and qualitative

planning which has similarities to Stake's model of evaluating antecedents, transactions and outcomes. The six models can be presented in tabular form to address issues outlined earlier in the chapter which curriculum planners planning evaluations should address (Table 7.3). If models are utilized as focusing tools for elements of curriculum planning and evaluation and as ways of drawing together key elements embraced by the term 'evaluation', then they serve their purpose. If they clarify issues in planners' minds then they are useful. The danger in using models lies in adopting an unreflective stance to them, using them prescriptively and inappropriately. The reflective teacher must sort and select, sift and balance, weigh and decide on which models or elements of models are relevant, appropriate and, above all, useful in planning curricula in the light of critical awareness of problems, possibilities, constraints and freedoms. If evaluation is to be fully integrated into curriculum planning then a measure of rigour and professional insight brought about by developing evaluation has to be cultivated by curriculum planners.

CONCLUSION

In the early part of this book the curriculum is viewed as a proposal for what children should learn and it is suggested that this proposal should be rooted in an analysis of the many constraints and influences exerted on it. Planners, it is argued, need to be constantly evaluating and changing their proposals in the light of the changing nature of the influences. Evaluation and planning are seen to exist in symbiosis and to spawn curriculum change, innovation and development. Hence the task for the curriculum planner is both philosophical and practical, asking what children should learn, why they should learn it and how they should learn it.

Planners are required to be analysts of ideologies – political and educational – epistemologies, sociologies, cultures, psychologies, managements and organizations, and evaluators of how these influences relate to the primary curriculum. Their twin role places them in a position which is both powerful and vulnerable depending on who they happen to be. If the planner is a powerful national agency, for example, the DES, then they can deploy a range of strategies to ensure that their proposals reach the schools through control of resources and through legislation. The use of power–coercive strategies coupled with empirical–rational and normative–re-educative strategies combine political and educational will to constitute a formidable force for planned educational change (Bennis, Benne and Chin, 1969). Clear evidence of this is the continuing debate and legislation on a common or national curriculum (DES, 1987), national monitoring and 'benchmark' testing at seven, eleven and fourteen years (ibid.) – all in the face of considerable professional hostility to such ideas (Saunders, 1987): the urge to appraise teachers; the strengthening of the

174

links between vocationalism, training and education; TVEI at secondary school level and CDT courses which extend down to the infant age range; the elevation of science and technology to one of the 'basics'; the erosion or dismantling of the power of the local education authorities; and the return to basics advocated in certain political quarters.

Against such force the planner at local or institutional level is perhaps disempowered to do anything but comply with national policies. Alternatively, one can argue that it is at an institutional level ultimately that decision-making and curriculum change in fact happens. Hence teachers, either individually or collectively, become powerful mediators of national prescriptions, accepting, adapting or perhaps resisting external pressures which they feel run counter to children's best interests. Teachers as curriculum planners thus become critical agents in defending or challenging political nostrums which underpin educational practices. In their dealings with children, then, teachers can become the 'transformative intellectuals' of critical theory (Giroux, 1986), awakening in children an awareness of inequalities, political and ideological hegemony in the social system with a view to changing society, or they can operate as agents of social, cultural and economic reproduction. This, however, is the substance of another book.

Here the notion can be established of teachers as curriculum planners, a notion which underscores the rationale of this book. The thrust of the discussion about planning which has occupied this book has been rooted in a double premiss. First, that curriculum planning requires 'reflective' teachers who can stand back and consider the various components of the curriculum process. Second, this calls for teachers to reflect on their practices from a basis of theory. The double premiss is interesting for it throws into relief the whole theory and practice relationship, a divide which persists between academics and teachers and their perspectives of each other (Downey and Kelly, 1979). The arguments and tenor of this book reject the necessity for that divide (c.f. Hirst, 1983). For 'extended' rather than 'restricted' professionality (Hoyle, 1975b) both theoreticians and practitioners need to lengthen their perspectives to embrace each others' domains. Theoreticians need to ground their theories in practice (Glaser and Strauss, 1967) and to open dialogue with practitioners if they are to do more than offer arid research or prescription.

Practitioners need conceptual tools to unearth the vagaries of the curriculum garden; it is insufficient for them to plan or support their planning by intuition, hunch or prejudice. Rather they should adopt a 'teacher as researcher' model (Stenhouse, 1975) which requires them to develop a willingness to examine systematically and rigorously their own practices and principles. This may prevent the educational myopia which surrounds both academicians and many classrooms.

To do justice to the notion of theory and practice existing in symbiosis, the curriculum planner for the primary school has to recognize that the task draws on ideas which by their range and scope are understandably daunting. Planning, as expressed here, will draw on macro and micro situational contexts, values, curriculum theory and evaluation if it is to be effective. While no simple solutions can reduce or replace the need to address this spread of concerns, the task can be facilitated in practice by planners involving themselves in dialogue, communication, debate and mutual support. The management of planning and implementation figures significantly here. Too frequently management practices, wittingly or not, frustrate or subvert the development of reflective planning through: inadequate sharing of responsibility; lack of time (Fullan, 1982); lack of discussion and communication; lack of resource use; lack of support — both at an institutional and an in-service level; an atmosphere or ethos marked by closure rather than openness to self-critical analysis; a leadership style which divides rather than unites staff and which diminishes morale; a poor capacity to solve or resolve problems; and a preoccupation (for whatever reason) with the pragmatic at the expense of the principle (Alexander, 1984).

If curriculum planning is to be thorough then the 'organizational health' (Miles, 1965) of the institution should be robust. Extended professionality, reflexivity, organizational health and collegiality are essential items if planning is to be able to embrace the many current constraints on the curriculum. Education is witnessing an unhappy dialogue between centralists and devolutionists, politicians and educators; the role of LEAs in curriculum planning and development is becoming increasingly unclear and increasingly threatened (DES, 1987); education is becoming more overtly political and politicized; pressure as never before is being put on teachers for the inclusion and exclusion of curriculum content; the breadth of the primary ethos is being jeopardized by conservative lobbies and instrumental ideologies, benchmark testing and back to basics; the role of teachers as agents or recipients of curriculum planning is ill-defined; curriculum debate is being marked by exhortation and power rather than reasoned argument.

Assessment-driven curricula replace situationally derived, experiential, and process-driven curricula. The proposals for a national curriculum represent a significant threat both to the notion of the primary ethos established at the beginning of the book and to the breadth of the curriculum which primary education has taken years to develop. The terms of the national curriculum are in many ways antithetical to the best elements of the primary curriculum; in their advocacy of 'subjects' (DES, 1987, p. 6) inappropriate models for young children's curricula are being adopted (Saunders, 1987); in their prioritizing of mathematics, English and science as 'core' subjects with the 'majority of curriculum time' (DES, 1987, p. 6) devoted to them, and with technology, history, geography, art, music and physical education given second-class status — with other experiences not even registering in the calculus — the best of the developing primary tradition of breadth, flexibility, responsiveness and negotiation risks being crowded out in the unholy rush to serve political expediency, and threatens to turn back the educational clock generations.

The aesthetic development of children, increasingly essential in an age which robs society of its humanity, is seen as an expendable element in a technological world (Eisner, 1985). It is on teachers that the onus falls to resist or subvert such moves. They need to be able to articulate the debate in order to preserve the best of the primary tradition. The argument through this book has been that the curriculum and the curriculum debate cannot afford to turn back the clock; the best of the past has to be taken to the future; there has to be a maintained balance between change and stability, reason and rhetoric, agency and determinism, technology and humanity, passive acceptance or contestation and debate. The issues raised in this book have attempted to map the terms of that debate.

BIBLIOGRAPHY

Adelman, C. (1984) The politics of evaluating, in M. Skilbeck (ed.) *Evaluating the Curriculum in the Eighties,* Hodder and Stoughton, Sevenoaks.

Alexander, R. (1984) *Primary Teaching*, Holt, Rinehart and Winston, Eastbourne.

Apple, M. (1982) *Education and Power*, Routledge and Kegan Paul, London.

Aries, P. (1973) *Centuries of Childhood*, Penguin, Harmondsworth.

Ashton, P., Kneen, P. and Davies, F. (1975) *The Aims of Primary Education: a Study of Teachers' Opinions*, Macmillan, London.

Bantock, G. H. (1975) Towards a theory of popular education, in M. Golby, J. Greenwald and R. West (eds.) *Curriculum Design*, Croom Helm and the Open University Press, London.

Bantock, G. H. (1976) Quality and equality in curricular provision, appendix one, in M. Skilbeck, Ideologies and values. Unit three, E203, *Curriculum Design and Development*, Open University Press, Milton Keynes.

Bantock, G. H. (1980) *Dilemmas of the Curriculum*, M. Robertson Publishers, Oxford.

Barnes, D. (1982) *Practical Curriculum Study*, Routledge and Kegan Paul, London.

Barrett, T. C. (1972) Taxonomy of the cognitive and affective dimensions of reading comprehension, in A. Melnik and J. Merritt (eds.) *Reading: Today and Tomorrow*, University of London Press.

Barrow, R. (1984) *Giving Teaching Back to Teachers*, Wheatsheaf Books, Sussex.

Barrow, R. and Woods, R. (1982) *An Introduction to Philosophy of Education (Second edition)*, Methuen, London.

Bennett, S. N. (1976) *Teaching Styles and Pupil Progress*, Open Books, London.

Bennett, S. N., Andreae, J., Hegarty, P. and Wade, B. (1980) *Open Plan Schools: Teaching, Curriculum, Design*, NFER, Slough.

Bennett, S. N., Desforges, C. and Wilkinson, E. (1984) *The Quality of Pupil Learning Experience*, Lawrence Erlbaum, London.

Bennis, W. G., Benne, K. D. and Chin, R. (1969) *The Planning of Change*, Holt, Rinehart and Winston, New York.

178

Bernstein, B. (1971) On the classification and framing of educational knowledge, in M. Young (ed.) *Knowledge and Control*, Collier Macmillan, London.

Bernstein, B. (1977) Class and pedagogies: visible and invisible, in B. Bernstein (ed.) *Class, Codes and Control*, Routledge and Kegan Paul, London.

Blenkin, G. and Kelly, A. V. (1981) *The Primary Curriculum*, Harper and Row, London.

Bloom, B. (ed.) (1956) *Taxonomy of Educational Objectives Handbook 1: Cognitive Domain*, Longman, London.

Blyth, W. A. L. (1965) *English Primary Education, Vol. 1*, Routledge and Kegan Paul, London.

Blyth, W. A. L. *et al.* (1976) *Place, Time and Society 8–13; Curriculum Planning in History, Geography and Social Science*, Collins and ESL Bristol, Glasgow and Bristol.

Blyth, W. A. L. and Derricot, R. (1985) Continuities and discontinuities in the primary curriculum, *Curriculum*, Vol. 6, No. 2 pp. 19–24.

Bobbitt, F. (1918) *The Curriculum*, Houghton Mifflin, Boston, Mass.

Borich, G. (1977) *The Appraisal of Teaching*, Addison-Wesley, Wokingham, Berks.

Boyson, R. and Cox, C. B. (eds.) (1975) *The Black paper 1975: The Fight for Education*, Dent, London.

Brink, T. D. (1983) Evaluation: a practical guide for teachers, quoted in L. Cohen and L. Manion (eds.) *A Guide to Teaching practice (Second Edition)*, Methuen and Co, London.

Brogden, M. (1983) Open plan primary schools: rhetoric and reality, *School Organization*, Vol. 3, No. 1, pp. 27–31.

Brown, M. and Precious, N. (1968) *The Integrated Day in the Primary School*, Ward Lock Educational, London.

Brubacher, J. S. (1962) *Modern Philosophies of Education*, McGraw Hill, New York.

Bruner, J. S. (1960) *The Process of Education*, Vintage Books, Random House, New York.

Bruner, J. S. (1966) *Towards a Theory of Instruction*, Harvard University Press, Cambridge, Massachusetts.

Bruner, J. S. (1970) Some theorems on instruction, in E. Stones (ed.) *Readings in Educational Psychology*, Methuen, London.

Bruner, J. S. (1974) *Beyond the Information Given*, Allen and Unwin, London.

Bush, T. (1986) *Theories of Educational Management*, Harper and Row, London.

Callaghan, J. (1976) Towards a national debate, *Education*, Vol. 148, No. 17, pp. 332–3.

Campbell, R. J. (1985) *Developing the Primary School Curriculum*, Holt Saunders, Eastbourne.

Carson, A. S. (1984) Control of the Curriculum – a case for teachers, *Journal of Curriculum Studies*, Vol. 16, No. 1, pp. 19–28.

Carter, S. and Hooley, G. J. (1983) The matching of learning environments to learning objectives – an empirical investigation, *Journal of Further and Higher Education*, Vol. 7, No. 2, pp. 221–40.

Cave, R. G. (1971) *An Introduction to Curriculum Development*, Ward Lock Educational, London.

Central Advisory Council for Education (1967) *Children and Their Primary Schools* (Plowden Report), HMSO, London.

Centre for Contemporary Cultural Studies (1981) *Unpopular Education*, Hutchinson, London.

Charters, W. W. (1924) *Curriculum Construction*, Macmillan, New York.

Clemson, D. (1983) Zen and the art of evaluation, *Insight*, Vol. 6, No. 2, pp. 77–81.

Clift, P., Weiner, G. and Wilson, E. (1981) *Record Keeping in Primary Schools*, Macmillan Educational, London.

Cooper, K. (1976) Curriculum evaluation – definition and boundaries, in D. Tawney (ed.) *Curriculum Evaluation Today: Trends and Implications*, Macmillan, London.

Cox, C. B. and Dyson, A. E. (1971) *The Black Papers on Education*, Davis-Poynter Ltd, London.

Cronbach, L. (1963) Course improvement through evaluation, *Teachers College Record*, Vol. 64, pp. 672–83.

Curriculum Development Centre (1980) *Core Curriculum for Australian Schools*, Curriculum Development Centre, Canberra.

Dalin, P. (1978) *Limits to Educational Change*, Macmillan, London.

Dalin, P. and Rust, V. D. (1983) *Can Schools Learn?* NFER-Nelson, Windsor.

Davies, I. K. (1976) *Objectives in Curriculum Design*, McGraw-Hill, Maidenhead.

Davis, E. (1983) *Teachers as Curriculum Evaluators*, Allen and Unwin, London.

Day, C., Johnston, D. and Whitaker, P. (1985) *Managing Primary Schools: A Professional Development Approach*, Harper and Row, London.

Dearden, R. F. (1968) *The Philosophy of Primary Education*, Routledge and Kegan Paul, London.

Department of Education and Science (1974) *A Language for Life* (Bullock Report), HMSO, London.

Department of Education and Science (1977) *Curriculum 11–16*, HMSO, London.

Department of Education and Science (1978a) *Primary Education in England*, HMSO, London.

Department of Education and Science (1978b) *Special Educational Needs: Report of the Committee of Enquiry into the Education of Handicapped Children and Young People* (Warnock Report), Cmnd. 7212, HMSO, London.

Department of Education and Science (1981) *The School Curriculum*, HMSO, London.

Department of Education and Science (1982a) *Mathematics Counts* (Cockcroft Report), HMSO, London.

Department of Education and Science (1982b) *Education 5–9: an Illustrative Survey of 80 First Schools*, HMSO, London.

Department of Education and Science (1982c) *The New Teacher in School*, HMSO, London.

Department of Education and Science (1983a) *9–13 Middle Schools*, HMSO, London.

Department of Education and Science (1983b) *Aesthetic Development*, HMSO, London.

Department of Education and Science (1985a) *English from 5 to 16, Curriculum Matters 1*, HMSO, London.

Department of Education and Science (1985b) *The Curriculum from 5–16, Curriculum Matters 2*, HMSO, London.

Department of Education and Science (1985c) *Better Schools*, Cmnd. 9469, HMSO, London.
Department of Education and Science (1985d) *Science 5–16*, HMSO, London.
Department of Education and Science (1985e) *Home Economics from 5 to 16, Curriculum Matters 5*, HMSO, London.
Department of Education and Science (1985f) *Health Education from 5 to 16, Curriculum Matters 6*, HMSO, London.
Department of Education and Science (1985g) *Quality in Schools: Evaluation and Appraisal*, HMSO, London.
Department of Education and Science (1987) *The National Curriculum 5–16: a Consultation Document*, HMSO London.
Donaldson, M. (1978) *Children's Minds*, Fontana, London.
Downey, M. and Kelly, A. V. (1979) *Theory and Practice of Education (Second Edition)*, Harper and Row, London.
Eggleston, J. (1977) *The Sociology of the School Curriculum*, Routledge and Kegan Paul, London.
Eggleston, J. and Kerry, T. (1985) Integrated studies, in S. N. Bennett and C. Desforges (eds.), *Recent Advances in Classroom Research, British Journal of Educational Psychology* Monograph Series no. 2, Scottish Academic Press, Edinburgh.
Eisner, E. (1975) Instructional and expressive objectives, in M. Golby, J. Greenwald and R. West (eds.) *Curriculum Design*, Croom Helm and the Open University Press, London.
Eisner, E. (1979) *The Educational Imagination*, Collier-Macmillan, London.
Eisner, E. (1985) *The Art of Educational Evaluation*, Falmer, Lewes, Sussex.
Eliot, T. S. (1948) *Notes Towards the Definition of Culture*, Faber, London.
Elliott, J. and Adelman, C. (1976) Innovation at the classroom level: a case study of the Ford Teaching Project, Unit 28, E203, *Curriculum Design and Development*, Open University Press, Milton Keynes.
Elliott-Kemp, J. and Williams, G. L. (1979) *The DION Handbook: Diagnosis of Individual and Organisational Needs for Staff Development and In-Service Training in Schools*, Sheffield Polytechnic.
Entwistle, H. (1970) *Child Centred Education*, Methuen, London.
Entwistle, H. (1981) Work, leisure and life styles, in B. Simon and W. Taylor (eds.) *Education in the Eighties*, Batsford, London.
Eraut, M. (1984) Institution-based curriculum evaluation, in M. Skilbeck (ed.) *Evaluating the Curriculum in the Eighties*, Hodder and Stoughton, Sevenoaks.
Everard, K. B. and Morris, G. (1985) *Effective School Management*, Harper and Row, London.
Flew, A. G. N. (1971) *An Introduction to Western Philosophy*, Thames and Hudson, London.
Fullan, M. (1982) *The Meaning of Educational Change*, Teachers College Press, New York.
Galton, M. and Simon, B. (1980) *Progress and Performance in the Primary Classroom*, Routledge and Kegan Paul, London.
Galton, M., Simon, B. and Croll, P. (1980) *Inside the Primary Classroom*, Routledge and Kegan Paul, London.

Giroux, H. (1983) *Theory and Resistance in Education*, Heinemann, London.

Giroux, H. (1986) Teacher education and the politics of engagement: the case for democratic schooling, *Harvard Educational Review*, Vol. 53 No. 3, pp. 213–38.

Glaser, B. and Strauss, A. (1967) *The Discovery of Grounded Theory*, Aldine, Chicago.

Glaser, R. (1977) Evaluation of instruction and changing educational models, in D. Hamilton, D. Jenkins, C. King, B. MacDonald and M. Parlett (eds.) *Beyond the Numbers Game*, Macmillan Basingstoke.

Glass, G. V. (1975) Comments on Professor Bloom's paper, cited in L. Stenhouse, *An Introduction to Curriculum Research and Development*, Heinemann, London.

Gronlund, N. E. (1974) *Determining Accountability for Classroom Instruction*, Collier-Macmillan, London.

Gross, N., Giacquinta, J. B. and Bernstein, M. (1971) *Implementing Organizational Innovations,* Harper and Row, New York.

Hall, G. E., Loucks, S. F., Rutherford, W. L. and Newlove, B. W. (1975) Levels of use of the innovation: a framework for analysing innovation adoption, *Journal of Teacher Education*, Vol. 26, No. 1, pp. 52–6.

Halpin, A. W. (1966) *Theory and Research in Administration*, Macmillan, New York.

Hargreaves, D. H. (1972) *Interpersonal Relations and Education*, Routledge and Kegan Paul, London.

Harlen, W. (1971) Some practical points in favour of curriculum evaluation, *Journal of Curriculum Studies*, Vol. 3, No. 2, pp. 128–34.

Harlen, W. (1980) Matching, in C. Richards (ed.) *Primary Education: Issues for the Eighties*, A. & C. Black, London.

Harlen, W. (1983) Evaluating the curriculum, in A. Paisey (ed.) *The Effective Teacher in Primary and Secondary Schools*, Ward Lock Educational, London.

Harlen, W. and Elliott, J. (1982) A checklist for planning or reviewing an evaluation, in R. McCormick (ed.) *Calling Education to Account*, Heinemann and the Open University Press, London.

Harrow, A. J. A. (1984) Taxonomy of the psychomotor domain, cited in J. Wiles and J. C. Bondi, *Curriculum Development; a Guide to Practice (second edition)*, Charles E. Merrel Publishing, Columbus, Ohio.

Hartnett, A. and Naish, M. (1976) *Theory and Practice of Education (Vol. one)*, Heinemann, London.

Harwood, D. (1985) We need political not Political Education for 5–13 year olds, *Education 3–13*, Vol. 13, No. 1, pp. 12–17.

Hatton, E. J. (1985) Team teaching in open-plan classrooms: innovation or regression? *School Organization*, Vol. 5, No. 2, pp. 203–9.

Havelock, R. (1973) *The Change Agents Guide to Innovation in Education*, Educational Technology Publications, Englewood Cliffs, New Jersey.

Hewlett, M. (1986) *Curriculum to Serve Society: How Schools Can Work for People*, Newstead Publishing, Loughborough.

Hicks, H. G. (1972) *The Management of Organizations; a Systems and Human Resources Approach (second edition)*, McGraw Hill, New York.

Higginbottom, P. J. (1976) Aims of education, in D. I. Lloyd (ed.) *Philosophy and the Teacher*, Routledge and Kegan Paul, London.

Hirst, P. H. (1965) Liberal education and the nature of knowledge, in R. D.

Archamboult (ed.) *Philosophical Analysis and Education*, Routledge and Kegan Paul, London.

Hirst, P. H. (1967) The logical and psychological aspects of teaching a subject, in R. S. Peters (ed.) *The Concept of Education*, Routledge and Kegan Paul, London.

Hirst, P. H. (1968) *The contribution of philosophy to the study of the curriculum*, in J. F. Kerr (ed.) *Changing the Curriculum*, University of London Press.

Hirst, P. H. (1975) The curriculum and its objectives – a defence of peicemeal rational planning, *The Doris Lee Lectures*, University of London Press.

Hirst, P. H. (1980) The logic of curriculum development, in M. Galton (ed.) *Curriculum Change: the Lessons of a Decade*, University of Leicester Press.

Hirst, P. H. (1983) Educational theory, in P. H. Hirst (ed.) *Educational Theory and Its Foundation Disciplines*, Routledge and Kegan Paul, London.

Hirst, P. H. and Peters, R. S. (1970) *The Logic of Education*, Routledge and Kegan Paul, London.

Holt, M. (1981) *Evaluating the Evaluators*, Hodder and Stoughton, Sevenoaks.

House, E. (1976) The conscience of educational evaluation, quoted in D. Jenkins, Towards evaluation, Unit 19, E203, *Curriculum Design and Development*, Open University Press, Milton Keynes.

House, E. (1977) Context and justification, in D. Hamilton, D. Jenkins, C. King, B. MacDonald, M. Parlett (eds.) *Beyond the Numbers Game*, Macmillan, Basingstoke.

House, E. R. (ed.) (1986) *New Directions in Educational Evaluation*, Falmer, Lewes.

Hoyle, E. (1971) How does the curriculum change? In R. Hooper (ed.) *The Curriculum: Context, Design and Development*, Oliver and Boyd, Edinburgh.

Hoyle, E. (1975a) The creativity of the school in Britain, in A. Harris, M. Lawn and W. Prescott (eds.) *Curriculum Innovation*, Croom Helm and the Open University Press, London.

Hoyle, E. (1975b) Creativity in the school, cited in L. Stenhouse, *An Introduction to Curriculum Research and Development*, Heinemann, London.

Hoyle, E. (1976) Strategies of curriculum change, Unit 23, E203, *Curriculum Design and Development*, Open University Press, Milton Keynes.

Huberman, M. and Miles, M. (1984) *Qualitative Data Analysis*, Sage Publications, Beverley Hills.

Ing, M. (1981) Motivation and curriculum planning, in P. Gordon *et al.* (eds.) *The Study of the Curriculum*, Batsford, London.

Inner London Education Authority, (1981) *The Study of Places in the Primary School*, ILEA Curriculum Guidelines, ILEA, London.

James, C. (1968) *Young Lives at Stake*, Collins, London.

Jenkins, D. (1975) Classic and romantic in the curriculum landscape, in M. Golby, J. Greenwald and R. West (eds.) *Curriculum Design*, Croom Helm and the Open University Press, London.

Jenkins, D. (1976) Man: a course of study, part 3 of Design issues, Units 14 and 15, E203, *Curriculum Design and Development*, Open University Press, Milton Keynes.

Jenkins, E. (1987) Philosophical flaws, *Times Educational Supplement*, 2 January.

Kamii, C. (1975) Pedagogical principles derived from Piaget's theory: relevance for educational practice, in M. Golby, J. Greenwald and R. West (eds.) *Curriculum Design*, Croom Helm and the Open University Press, London.

Kelly, A. V. (ed.) (1980) *Curriculum Context*, Harper and Row, London.

Kelly, A. V. (1982) *The Curriculum: Theory and Practice (second edition)*, Harper and Row, London.

Kelly, A. V. (1986) *Knowledge and Curriculum Planning*, Harper and Row, London.

Kemmis, S. (1982) Seven principles for programme evaluation in curriculum development and innovation, *Journal of Curriculum Studies*, Vol. 14, No. 3, pp. 221–40.

Kerr, J. F. (1968) *Changing the Curriculum*, University of London Press.

Kerry, T. and Sands, M. (1982) *Handling Classroom Groups*, Macmillan, London.

King, R. (1978) *All Things Bright and Beautiful? A Sociological Study of Infants' Classrooms*, Wiley, Chichester.

Kohl, H. R. (1970) *The Open Classroom*, Methuen, London.

Krathwohl, D., Bloom, B. and Masia, B. (1956) *Taxonomy of Educational Objectives, Handbook Two, Affective Domain*, Longmans, London.

Lacey, C. and Lawton, D. (eds.) (1981) *Issues in Evaluation and Accountability*, Methuen, London.

Lancashire County Council (1981) *Lancashire Looks at... Science in the Primary School*, Lancashire County Council Education Department, Preston.

Langford, G. (1968) *Philosophy and Education*, Macmillan, London.

Lavelle, M. (1984) The role of consultancy in curriculum and organisation development innovation in education, *School Organization*, Vol. 4, No. 2, pp. 161–9

Lawton, D. (1973) *Social Change, Educational Theory and Curriculum Planning*, University of London Press.

Lawton, D. (1980) *The Politics of the School Curriculum*, Routledge and Kegan Paul, London.

Lawton, D. (1983) *Curriculum Studies and Educational Planning*, Hodder and Stoughton, Sevenoaks.

Lawton, D. (1984) *The Tightening Grip: Growth of Central Control of the School Curriculum*, Bedford Way Papers 21, University of London Press.

Lawton, D. (ed.) (1986) *School Curriculum Planning*, Hodder and Stoughton, Sevenoaks.

Lewy, A. (1977) *Handbook of Curriculum Evaluation*, UNESCO, Longmans, New York.

Lortie, D. (1975) Innovation and the authority structure of the school, in A. Harris, M. Lawn and W. Prescott (eds.) *Curriculum Innovation*, Croom Helm and the Open University Press, London.

Loubser, J. J., Spiers, H. and Moody, C. (1975) Case studies of educational innovation: at the regional level, cited in L. Stenhouse, *An Introduction to Curriculum Research and Development*, Heinemann, London.

MacDonald, B. (1975) Innovation and incompetence, cited in L. Stenhouse, *An Introduction to Curriculum Research and Development*, Heinemann, London.

MacDonald, B. (1976) Evaluation and control of education, in D. Tawney (ed.), *Curriculum Evaluation Today: Trends and Implications*, Macmillan, London.

MacDonald, B. (1977) A political classification of evaluation studies, in D. Hamilton, D. Jenkins, C. King, B. MacDonald, M. Parlett (eds.) *Beyond the Numbers Game*, Macmillan, Basingstoke.

MacDonald, B. (1982) Who's afraid of evaluation? in C. Richards (ed.) *New Directions in Primary Education*, Falmer, Lewes, Sussex.

MacDonald-Ross, M. (1975) Behavioural objectives: a critical review, in M. Golby, J. Greenwald and R. West (eds.) *Curriculum Design*, Croom Helm, London.

Mager, R. F. (1962) *Preparing Instructional Objectives*, Fearon Publishers, Belmont, California.

Mannheim, K. (1936) *Ideology and Utopia*, Routledge and Kegan Paul, London.

McCormick, R. and James, M. (1983) *Curriculum Evaluation in Schools*, Croom Helm, London.

Meighan, R. (1981) *A Sociology of Educating*, Holt, Rinehart and Winston, Eastbourne.

Miles, M. (1965) Planned change and organisational health: figure and ground, in R. O. Carlson (ed.) *Change Processes in the Public Schools*, University of Oregon Press.

Morrison, K. R. B. (1984) Improving reading comprehension: approaches and practices, *Education 3–13*, Vol. 12, No. 2, pp. 14–20.

Morrison, K. R. B. (1985) Tensions in subject specialist teaching in primary schools, *Curriculum*, Vol. 6, No. 2, pp. 24–9.

Morrison, K. R. B. (1986a) Developing a framework for curriculum cohesion in primary teacher education, *Durham and Newcastle Research Review*, Vol. 10, No. 56, pp. 291–5.

Morrison, K. R. B. (1986b) Primary school subject specialists as agents of school-based curriculum change, *School Organization*, Vol. 6, No. 2, pp. 175–83.

Morrison, K. R. B. (1987) The curriculum from 5–16: a primary response, *Curriculum*, Vol. 8, No. 2, pp. 37–44.

Nisbet, J. (1983) Educational psychology, in P. Hirst (ed.) *Educational Theory and its Foundation Disciplines*, Routledge and Kegan Paul, London.

Norris, R. (1975) An examination of schedules of criteria related to teacher competence, *British Journal of Teacher Education*, Vol. 1, pp. 87–95.

Nuttall, D. (1981) *School Self-Evaluation: Accountability with a Human Face?*, Schools Council, London.

Oakeshott, M. (1976a) Rational conduct, cited in H. Sockett, *Designing the Curriculum*, Open Books, Shepton Mallett.

Oakeshott, M. (1976b) Rational conduct, quoted in H. Sockett, Approaches to curriculum planning, Unit 16, E203, *Curriculum Design and Development*, Open University Press, Milton Keynes.

Oliver, D. (1982) The primary curriculum: a proper basis for planning, in C. Richards (ed.) *New Directions in Primary Education*, Falmer, Lewes.

Open University (1980) *Curriculum in Action*, P234, Open University Press, Milton Keynes.

Oppenheim, A. N. (1966) *Questionnaire Design and Attitude Measurement*, Heinemann, London.

Orlosky, D. E. and Smith, B. O. (eds.) (1978) *Curriculum Development: Issues and Insights*, Rand McNally, Chicago.

Ormell, C. (1980) Values in education, in R. Straughan and J. Wrigley (eds.) *Values and Evaluation in Education*, Harper and Row, London.

Parlett, M. and Hamilton, D. (1976) Evaluation as illumination, in D. Tawney (ed.) *Curriculum Evaluation Today: Trends and Implications*, Macmillan, London.

Passmore, J. (1980) *The Philosophy of Teaching*, Duckworth, London.

Peters, R. S. (1966) *Ethics and Education*, Allen and Unwin, London.

Peters, R. S. (ed.) (1967) *The Concept of Education*, Routledge and Kegan Paul, London.

Peters, R. S. (1969) *Perspectives on Plowden*, Routledge and Kegan Paul, London.

Peters, R. S. (ed.) (1973) *Philosophy of Education*, Oxford University Press, London.

Peterson, A. D. C. (1975) Arts and science sides in the sixth form, cited in D. Lawton, *Class Culture and the Curriculum*, Routledge and Kegan Paul, London.

Phenix, P. (1975) Realms of meaning, in M. Golby, J. Greenwald and R. West (eds.) *Curriculum Design*, Croom Helm and the Open University Press, London.

Pinar, W. (ed.) (1975) *Curriculum Theorizing: the Reconceptualists*, McCutchon Publishing, Berkeley, California.

Pinar, W. and Grumet, M. (1981) Theory and practice and the reconceptualisation of curriculum studies, in M. Lawn and L. Barton (eds.) *Rethinking Curriculum Studies*, Croom Helm, London.

Pollard, A. (1985) *The Social World of the Primary School*, Holt, Rinehart and Winston, Eastbourne.

Pope, D. (1983) *The Objectives Model of Curriculum Planning*, Occasional Paper 10, Council for Educational Technology, London.

Popham, W. J. (1975) Systematic instruction, cited in M. MacDonald-Ross, Behavioural objectives: a critical review, in M. Golby, J. Greenwald and R. West (eds.) *Curriculum Design*, Croom Helm and the Open University Press, London.

Pring, R. (1973) Curriculum integration, in R. S. Peters (ed.) *The Philosophy of Education*, Oxford University Press.

Pring, R. (1976) *Knowledge and Schooling*, Open Books, Shepton Mallett.

Pring, R. (1984) The problems of confidentiality, in M. Skilbeck (ed.) *Evaluating the Curriculum in the Eighties*, Hodder and Stoughton, Sevenoaks.

Proctor, N. (1984) Criteria for a common curriculum, *Curriculum*, Vol. 5, No. 1, pp. 10–17.

Ridley, K. and Trembath, D. (1986) Primary school organization: some rhetoric and some reason, in Cohen A. and Cohen L. (eds.) *Primary Education: A Sourcebook for Teachers*, Harper and Row, London.

Ruddock, R. (1981) *Evaluation: a Consideration of Principles and Methods*, Manchester Monographs 10, University of Manchester.

Ryle, G. (1949) *The Concept of Mind*, Harmondsworth, Penguin.

Saunders, T. (ed.) (1987) *The National Curriculum Primary Questions*, Scholastic Publications, Leamington Spa.

Schmuck, R. T. and Miles, M. (1983) Organization development in schools, quoted in P. Dalin and V. D. Rust, *Can Schools Learn?* NFER-Nelson, Windsor.

Schofield, H. (1972) *The Philosophy of Education: An Introduction*, Allen and Unwin, London.

Schools Council (1972) *Exploration Man, an Introduction to Integrated Studies*, Oxford University Press.

Schools Council (1973) *With Objectives in Mind*, MacDonald, London.

Schools Council (1981) *The Practical Curriculum*, working paper 70, Methuen, London.

Schools Council (1983) *Primary Practice*, working paper 75, Methuen, London.

Schwab, J. (1975) Structure of the disciplines: meanings and significancies, in M. Golby, J. Greenwald and R. West (eds.) *Curriculum Design*, Croom Helm and the Open University Press, London.

Scrimshaw, P. (1976) Towards the whole curriculum, Units 9 and 10, E203, *Curriculum Design and Development*, Open University Press, Milton Keynes.

Scrimshaw, P. (1983) Educational ideologies, Unit 2, E204, *Purpose and Planning in the Curriculum*, Open University Press, Milton Keynes.

Scriven, M. (1967) The methodology of evaluation, in R. Tyler, R. Gagne and M. Scriven (eds.) *Perspectives on Curriculum Evaluation*, AERA Monograph Series on Curriculum Evaluation 1, Rand McNally, Chicago.

Scriven, M. (1976) Goal-free evaluation, cited in D. Jenkins, Six alternative models of curriculum evaluation, unit 20, E203, *Curriculum Design and Development*, Open University Press, Milton Keynes.

Sharp, R., Green, A. and Lewis, J. (1975) *Education and Social Control*, Routledge and Kegan Paul, London.

Siann, G. and Ugwuegbu, D. (1980) *Educational Psychology in a Changing World*, Allen and Unwin, London.

Simons, H, (1982a) Conversation piece: the practice of interviewing in case study research, in R. McCormick (ed.) *Calling Education to Account*, Heinemann and the Open University Press, London.

Simons, H. (1982b) Suggestions for a school self-evaluation based on democratic principles, in R. McCormick (ed.) *Calling Education to Account*, Heinemann and the Open University Press, London.

Simons, H. (1984) Issues in curriculum evaluation at the local level, in M. Skilbeck (ed.) *Evaluating the Curriculum in the Eighties*, Hodder and Stoughton, Sevenoaks.

Sivanandan, A. (1979) Imperialism and disorganic development in the silicon age, *Race and Class*, Vol. 21, No. 2, pp. 111–26.

Skilbeck, M. (1976a) Basic questions in curriculum, Unit 2, E203, *Curriculum Design and Development*, Open University Press, Milton Keynes.

Skilbeck, M. (1976b) The curriculum development process: a model for school use, appendix 2, Unit 7, E203, *Curriculum Design and Development*, Open University Press, Milton Keynes.

Skilbeck, M. (1982) School-based curriculum development, in V. Lee and D. Zeldin (eds.) *Planning in the Curriculum*, Hodder and Stoughton, Sevenoaks,

Skilbeck, M. (1984) *School-Based Curriculum Development*, Harper and Row, London.

Skilbeck, M. and Harris, A. (1976) Knowledge and understanding, Unit 4, E203, *Curriculum Design and Development*, Open University Press, Milton Keynes.

Smith, F. (1971) *Understanding Reading*, Holt, Rinehart and Winston, Eastbourne.

Smith, F. (1975) *Comprehension and Learning: a Conceptual Framework for Teachers*, Holt, Rinehart and Winston, Eastbourne.

Smith, F. (1978) *Reading*, Cambridge University Press.

Sockett, H. (1976) *Designing the Curriculum*, Open Books, Shepton Mallett.

Stake, R. E. (1976a) The countenance of educational evaluation, cited in D. Jenkins, Six alternative models of curriculum evaluation, Unit 20, E203, *Curriculum Design and Development*, Open University Press, Milton Keynes.

Stake, R. E. (1976b) Responsive evaluation, cited in D. Jenkins, Six alternative models of curriculum evaluation, Unit 20, E203, *Curriculum Design and Development*, Open University Press, Milton Keynes.

Stake, R. E. (1977a) Description versus analysis, in D. Hamilton, D. Jenkins, C. King, B. MacDonald, M. Parlett (eds.) *Beyond the Numbers Game*, Macmillan, Basingstoke.

Stake, R. E. (1977b) Formative and Summative evaluation, in D. Hamilton, D. Jenkins, C. King, B. MacDonald, M. Parlett (eds.) *Beyond the Numbers Game*, Macmillan, Basingstoke.

Stake, R. E. (1982) The methods of evaluating, in V. Lee and D. Zeldin (eds) *Planning in the Curriculum*, Hodder and Stoughton, Sevenoaks.

Stenhouse, L. (1968) The humanities curriculum project, *Journal of Curriculum Studies*, Vol. 1, pp. 26–33.

Stenhouse, L. (1975) *An Introduction to Curriculum Research and Development*, Heinemann, London.

Stewart, V. (1985) Change: the challenge for management, cited in K. B. Everard and G. Morris, *Effective School Management*, Harper and Row, London.

Stonier, T. (1982) Changes in Western society: educational implications, in C. Richards (ed.) *New Directions in Primary Education*, Falmer, Lewes.

Stubbs, M. and Delamont, S. (eds.) (1976) *Explorations in Classroom Observation*, John Wiley, Chichester.

Stufflebeam, D. L. (1976) Educational evaluation and decision making, cited in D. Jenkins, Six alternative models of curriculum evaluation, Unit 20, E203, *Curriculum Design and Development*, Open University Press, Milton Keynes.

Taba, H. (1962) *Curriculum Development: Theory and Practice*, Harcourt, Brace and World, New York.

Tannenbaum, R. and Schmidt, W. H. (1985) How to choose a leadership pattern, in K. B. Everard and G. Morris, *Effective School Management*, Harper and Row, London.

Taylor, D. B. (1976) Eeny, meeny, miney meaux: alternative evaluation models, *North Central Association Quarterly*, Vol. 50, No. 4, pp. 353–8.

Taylor, J. (1983) *Organizing and Integrating the First School Day*, Allen and Unwin, London.

Taylor, P. H. (1968) The contribution of psychology to the study of the curriculum, in J. Kerr (ed.) *Changing the Curriculum*, University of London Press.

Taylor, P. H. (1970) *How Teachers Plan Their Courses*, NFER, Slough.

Taylor, P. H. and Richards, C. (1979) *An Introduction to Curriculum Studies*, NFER, Slough.

Tickle, L. (1985) From class teachers to specialist teachers: curriculum continuity and school organization, in R. Derricot (ed.) *Curriculum Continuity: Primary to Secondary*, NFER-Nelson, Windsor.

Tyler, R. W. (1949) *Basic Principles of Curriculum and Instruction*, University of Chicago Press.

University of Leeds (1985) *The Curriculum from 5 to 16: a Primary Perspective*, University of Leeds School of Education.

Walker, J. (1981) Evaluation is a dicey business, *Curriculum*, Vol. 2, No. 2, pp. 41–6.

Walkerdine, V. (1983) It's only natural: rethinking child-centred pedagogy, in A. M. Wolpe and J. Donald (eds.) *Is There Anyone Here From Education?*, Pluto Press, London.

Waters, D. (1982) *Primary School Projects: Planning and Development*, Heinemann, London.

Weber, M. (1972) The Chinese literati, in B. Cosin (ed.) *Education, Structure and Society*, Penguin, Harmondsworth.

Westergaard, J. and Resler, H. (1976) *Class in a Capitalist Society*, Penguin, Harmondsworth.

Wheeler, D. K. (1967) *Curriculum Process*, University of London Press.

Whitaker, P. (1983) *The Primary Head*, Heinemann, London.

White, J. (1982a) The primary teacher as servant of the state, in C. Richards (ed.) *New Directions in Primary Education*, Falmer, Lewes.

White, J. (1982b) The curriculum mongers: education in reverse, in T. Horton and P. Raggart (eds.) *Challenge and Change in the Curriculum*, Hodder and Stoughton, Sevenoaks.

Whitehead, A.N. (1932) *The Aims of Education*, Ernest Benn, London.

Whitfield, R. (1980) Curriculum objectives: help or hindrance?, in M. Galton (ed.) *Curriculum Change: The Lessons of a Decade*, University of Leicester Press.

Whitty, G. (1985) *Sociology and School Knowledge*, Methuen, London.

Wicksteed, D. and Hill, M. (1979) Is this you? *Education 3–13*, Vol. 7, No. 1, pp. 32–6.

Wiles, J. and Bondi, J.C. (1984) *Curriculum Development: a Guide to Practice (second edition)*, Charles E. Merrill Publishing, Columbus, Ohio.

Wilson, A. (1983) From the specific to the general, *Times Higher Education Supplement*, 14 October.

Wilson, P. S. (1971) *Interest and Discipline in Education*, Routledge and Kegan Paul, London.

Wordsworth, W. (1966) Ode: intimations of immortality from recollections of early childhood, in *Selected poems of Wordsworth*, World's Classics series 189, Oxford University Press.

Worthington, E. (1884) *Rousseau's Emile*, D. C. Heath and Co, London.

Yeomans, A. (1983) Collaborative group work in primary and secondary schools: Britain and the USA, *Durham and Newcastle Research Review*, Vol. 10, No. 51, pp. 99–104.

AUTHOR INDEX

SUBJECT INDEX

193